This book is dedicated to the teenagers and adults with Asperger Syndrome who only want to be understood and understand.

Acknowledgements

I would like to acknowledge my husband, Bill, for his love and steadfast support for our thirty-three years of marriage. I want to acknowledge my three children—Craig, Scott and Blair—for making life exciting and worth living. I want to acknowledge my sweet grandson Craig for keeping me young. Additionally, I want to thank Laura Gardner, my research assistant, for her encouragement and helpful research, Kathryn Siconolfi and Steven Collier for their marvelous stories and Messiah College for providing student and faculty grants that helped facilitate this writing project.

441-657

NANCY J.

A Pra

This book is dedicated to the teen

adults with Asperger Syndrome :

want to be understood and under

Acknowledgements

I would like to acknowledge my husband, Bill, for his love and steadfast support for our thirty-three years of marriage. I want to acknowledge my three children—Craig, Scott and Blair—for making life exciting and worth living. I want to acknowledge my sweet grandson Craig for keeping me young. Additionally, I want to thank Laura Gardner, my research assistant, for her encouragement and helpful research, Kathryn Siconolfi and Steven Collier for their marvelous stories and Messiah College for providing student and faculty grants that helped facilitate this writing project.

Contents

Introduction

Asperger Syndrome and the Experiences of Teens and Adults

This book is written to provide practical strategies to help anyone who has a desire to improve his or her social skills, especially teenagers and adults with Asperger Syndrome (AS). It is also for those interested in learning about AS, the impact AS has on social situations, and those looking for strategies to support a teen or adult who wants to progress in this area.

The strategies in this book are based on principles gleaned from the biographies of adults with AS and autism. The writers overwhelmingly reveal that the social turn around in their lives came as a result of skillful observation, self-examination, analysis, implementation of personal strategies and ongoing evaluation.

In her co-authored book *Unwritten Rules of Social Relationships: Decoding Social Mysteries through the Unique Perspectives of Autism* Temple Grandin reports "my ability to function in the world and develop social relationships has been learned solely through my intellect—by becoming a very good social detective—and use of my visualization skills" (Grandin and Barron 2005, p.31). In her role as social detective Dr Grandin observed her social surroundings, taking note of the relevant details that made up each social situation, and recorded the observations in her memory for future reference. The observations allowed her to build an understanding of the social world and identify personal strategies to help her better manage social situations. It wasn't until she was an adult that she possessed enough information or data from her personal experiences to accurately interpret her social observations, but with maturity and an increased number of social experiences she progressed.

Co-author Sean Barron reports that his social turn around came after years of "listening, absorbing, watching and asking questions [seeking] to lose his naiveté and to develop some insight into human nature" (Grandin and Barron 2005, p.78). He describes his experience with autism as a painful journey. He always wanted to have social connectedness with other people, but this eluded him primarily because of his fears and inability to interpret the social intentions of others. His confidence and feeling at ease in social situations were not things he learned in a single "A-ha!" moment, but came over time as a result of a process (Grandin and Barron 2005). The process was slow and difficult, but with ongoing help from his parents he progressed. This approach worked well for Sean and in 2005 he wrote:

> Thankfully, the social connections I so desperately wanted growing up have been made. My relationship with my family is extraordinary. I have a network of wonderful friends, a job as a newspaper reporter that satisfies me on an intellectual level and a woman whom I've been dating since 2003. All the people in my life affect me in positive ways. (Grandin and Barron 2005, p.82)

From these authors we learn that "figuring out how to be socially competent is a slow process of continuous improvement. There are no sudden break-throughs, and there is no single social skills program that will make a child become socially aware" (Grandin and Barron 2005, p.36). Social relationships are too varied and complex to be "converted down to a final mathematical proof" (p.102).

In past generations it might have been possible to teach social skills in isolation with the expectation that the skills would apply to every situation over a lifetime, but that is not the case today. Social skills are less fixed than in previous generations. The loosening of social requirements has much to do with changing social values in many communities. Changes have always occurred, but are now occurring at a more rapid rate as a result of the expanding ability for people from different communities to interact and share their traditions through technology. Not only are social requirements changing rapidly, but so is the uniform application of social skills to all settings.

In the past social skills that were taught and expected in the home were the same as those expected at school and work, but that has changed. No longer are children required to address their parents with the same level of respect as their teachers or, in some cases, they are no longer required to respect their teachers as they would their parents. No longer are teens and adults required to refrain from swearing in every setting. At home or school this may be permissible, but not at work, for example.

Inconsistencies in social requirements can be seen regularly in television commercials and advertising. In a recent sales campaign by an international power drink company a photograph of a famous athlete sticking out his tongue is used to promote the product. In many communities sticking your tongue out is considered rude or immature. This sales image sends a mixed message to anyone trying to figure out appropriate social behavior. Of course, sticking out your tongue does get attention and this is good when you want people to remember your product. Unfortunately, this can be a problem for the child, teen, or adult who sticks out his or her tongue at school or work just trying to be hip or "fit-in."

With social rules changing and the consistent application of social skills in flux across all settings it is impossible to teach every social requirement for every social situation in every community. For these reasons this book does not focus a great deal of attention on teaching a specific list of social skills, but on the general capabilities that will allow you to identify and implement the social requirements of your home and community. These general capabilities are the disciplines of skillful observation, self-examination, analysis, implementation of personalized strategies, and ongoing evaluation.

If you are a teen or adult with AS you may be asking yourself the following questions at this point in the book:

- Why must I change?

- Why can't people accept me as I am?

- Why can't other people change?

- Isn't the point of disability awareness and advocacy to encourage the general public to become tolerant and embrace differences?

- Isn't the point to recognize that people think and behave differently and, in the case of AS, the world needs to accept "neurodiversity"?

The answers to these questions are mixed. Yes, the world is a better place because of diversity, yet the reality is that we are all responsible for our choices and behaviors that result in certain outcomes. If your social skills are poor and interfere with your interactions and relationships with others you may want to investigate strategies that can help increase your social capabilities. If you have tried to accomplish this in the past and have failed it is important to remember that progress is sometimes slow and in many situations noticeable change does not occur until early or middle adult life, but don't be discouraged because many teens and adults with AS have been able to strengthen their social competence with slow yet continuous progress. Choosing to work to improve social competence has the potential to lead to good outcomes like finding a satisfying job that lasts for many years, increasing your ability to live independently, and to acquire meaningful relationships, while the choice not to engage in efforts to improve social competence has the potential to lead to negative outcomes like unemployment, underemployment, increased dependence on others, and isolation.

Having a disability does not exonerate us from behaving our best. Social behaviors that hurt other people or behaviors that interfere with productivity on the job will not be embraced by the general public. The reality is that better social awareness and competence is more likely to lead to positive outcomes than choosing to do nothing.

Change in social behavior will be difficult. If it were easy it would just happen. But we know from the biographies of adults with AS and autism that progress is possible. This book promotes progress as the goal, not perfection.

It is important to remember that overcoming difficulties requires support from others. Sean Barron (Grandin and Barron 2005), acknowledged his parents as significant contributors in his social progress. When he was ready to explore and identify solutions for his social differences his parents were ready and assisted him by answering his questions and by providing for him the social perspective that was missing from his own skill set. This book is also written for those others—including parents, siblings, grandparents, teachers, counselors and therapists—who are willing and able to provide support to anyone who desires to make improvements in his or her social life.

A basic principle of instructional design states that all learning requires some prior knowledge, a mental set (or schema), that will provide "a meaningful framework within which to understand, interpret, and apply new learning" (Zook 2001, p.5). One way to establish this meaningful framework is through a common foundation and vocabulary. The common foundation and vocabulary required for new learning in the area of social skills begins with an understanding of AS.

WHAT IS ASPERGER SYNDROME?

Asperger Syndrome (AS) is one of several conditions found in a group of neurodevelopmental disabilities known as autism spectrum disorders (Klin, Volkmar and Sparrow 2000). People who have AS display qualitative impairment in social interactions in addition to having a tendency to engage in restricted and stereotyped patterns of behavior, interests and activities (American Psychiatric Association 2000).

Impairment in social interaction occurs in a variety of areas including interpreting and expressing nonverbal communication through eye contact, facial expression, body posture, and gestures; peer relationships; spontaneous seeking to share enjoyment, interests, or achievements with others; and social or emotional reciprocity.

Restricted, repetitive and stereotyped patterns of behavior, interests, and activities include:

- enthusiastic preoccupation with one or more stereotyped and restricted patterns of interest that is abnormal either in intensity or focus

- inflexible adherence to specific, nonfunctional routines or rituals such as stereotyped and repetitive motor mannerisms (e.g., hand or finger flapping or twisting, or complex whole-body movements)

- persistent preoccupation with parts of objects.

Many people with AS also experience physical problems that may include motor awkwardness, clumsiness and strong reactivity to sensations such as touch, sound, taste, smell, temperature, pain, and movement. These problems occur despite the gift of an average or above-average intellect.

In order for these difficulties to warrant a diagnosis of AS they must significantly interfere with the ability of the person to function in one or more of the major areas of life including social, learning, self-care, independence or work.

Hans Asperger (1906–1980) first wrote about the cluster of behavioral symptoms known today as Asperger Syndrome. He initially called the syndrome "Autisitschen Psychopathen im Kindesalter" which in English translates as "autistic psychopathology in childhood." Asperger identified a group of his patients who appeared to be weak or lacking in social relatedness, empathy, and ability to form friendships. His patients, who ranged in age from 5 to 35 years, also engaged in one-sided conversations; demonstrated intense, self-absorbed special interests and preoccupations; and displayed clumsy motor movements. He observed that the intense preoccupations provided pleasure, yet interfered with many other functions in life. Asperger was convinced that people diagnosed with AS could use their special interests and talents successfully in adulthood (Asperger 1991).

Asperger's work was reviewed and revised by renowned British psychiatrist Lorna Wing, and renamed Asperger Syndrome in 1981 (Frith 1991). The syndrome was renamed because the term "psychopathology" had become synonymous with antisocial behavior and was no longer appropriate for describing Asperger condition.

Autism spectrum disorders, as a category, occur in 1 in every 150 children in the United States (Center for Disease Control and Prevention 2007), 1 in every 116 children in the United Kingdom (Baird *et al.* 2006), 1 in every 165 children in Canada (Fombonne *et al.* 2006), 1 in every 160 in Australia (MacDermott *et al.* 2006) and are rising in prevalence in many other countries including Japan, Denmark and Sweden (Kurita 2006).

At this time there is no known cause of AS or autism, although researchers suspect that genetics is a major contributor. Researchers base this suspicion on monozygotic twin studies that reveal that identical twins have a much higher rate of autism than fraternal twins or singlet siblings. A recent study identified a recurrent genetic difference that substantially predicted a person's susceptibility to one type of autism that appears to account for approximately one percent of the cases of autism (Weiss *et al.* 2008).

There is no known cure for AS or autism; however, the impact of the disability can be reduced with early and ongoing intervention. This book will not cover the methodologies or practices of early intervention or those interventions used with children, but will focus on the principles and requirements of intervention for teenagers and adults.

The greatest requirement for social progress with teens and adults with AS is that they choose to participate in the intervention. It is the premise of this book that, in order for any social progress to be made, the person must recognize a need for change, be able and willing to observe his or her social surroundings, be willing to reflect upon the observations, and then select and implement personalized strategies to meet his or her individual needs. If initial efforts fail, the person needs to modify his or her approach and continue trying. All of this can be realized with help and support from family, friends, teachers, counselors, and therapists.

In order to understand the impact of AS on social skills, social competency and social relatedness, it is critical to expand the mental set that you have now constructed to include specific experiences of teens and adults living with this disability.

EXPERIENCES OF TEENS AND ADULTS WITH ASPERGER SYNDROME

The life experiences of teens and adults with AS are as varied as those of any group of people, but there are common experiences. These common experiences stem from the challenges that occur when living in a highly prescribed social world without the skills necessary to navigate social relationships.

Before moving into the specific social experiences, it is important to take a look at what is meant by the terms "teenager" and "adult."

Who are teenagers?

Teenagers are young people between the ages of 13 and 19 years. This is the transitional stage in life that occurs between childhood and adulthood and is also known as adolescence. Adolescence is a time of physical, psychological, and social change.

Physical changes include puberty, which is the process of sexual maturation. In addition to sexual maturation adolescence is a time of great overall physical change in height, weight, and features. This period of rapid growth occurs as a direct result of the internal release of hormones. Hormones are "a substance, usually a peptide or steroid, produced by one tissue and conveyed by the bloodstream to another, to effect physiological activity, such as growth or metabolism" (American Heritage® Dictionary of the English language 2008). Hormones in large quantities cause rapid physiological change that can cause a teen to feel uneasy and unsure. The rapid physical changes can also cause discomfort and a great deal of confusion in identity, especially for the young person with AS who finds comfort in predictability and sameness.

The psychological changes that occur during adolescence involve both cognitive and emotional growth. The most notable change in teenagers is the increased ability to cope with situations and solve problems of increasing complexity. This capacity to solve problems at increasingly complex levels can at times be masked by the emotional overload experienced during this time of change, but it is occurring and will be more evident once the teen becomes settled with his or her physical and emotional changes.

The social changes that occur during adolescence are very much related to the sexual and physical changes. Teenagers are becoming more interested in social relationships and being socially accepted. Teenagers are more apt to place increased importance on peers and friends over parents or guardians. This is true for the majority of teens including those with AS. This is true for those teens who do not have friends, yet want to have friends, and for those who choose not to have friends. This is a time when an increased awareness in peer social behavior is evident. It may not be evident by an increased number of social contacts, as with teens who do not have social difficulties, but will be revealed by an increased interest in teen clothing, make-up, hair styles, music, teen- or young-adult hobbies, interacting with others on the internet, and noticing the opposite sex.

During adolescence social changes will include the search for a unique identity and increased understanding of oneself. Teenagers often ask questions like:

- Who am I?

- Who do I want to be?

- What do I want to do with my life?

- Am I a good person?

- Do other people like me or find me attractive?

- Why don't kids like me?

Adolescence is a time when development within the individual drives or, or in some cases, eases him or her towards an increased desire for independence in everyday life. This stage seems to propel the majority of teens to be more social than at any other time in their lives. This is a good time to focus on increasing social competency, although intense focus in this area might be more successful if addressed in the later teen years for the person with AS. Since adolescence is such a tumultuous and confusing time for everyone, the actual freedom to explore social relationships may best be addressed after the physical, emotional, and psychological changes become established and the physiology settles down. This may be especially true for those who struggle with sensory integration, emotional regulation, and a strong need for sameness.

Who are adults?

Adults are people who have reached physical maturity and who are considered by their society as having reached the age of majority, which is the legal term for the age when children can legally assume control over their lives including their actions and decisions. It is at this point that parents or guardians are no longer legally responsible for the person. With the decrease in parental control this is also a time in life for increased independence. This is a hard transition for many people, but can be particularly difficult for anyone with a disability since living independently requires many capabilities.

The transition to adulthood can also be a difficult time for parents and guardians of an adult with a disability who may be concerned or overly concerned that their adult child will not be able to live on his or her own without support. It can be hard for parents and guardians to "let go" of their adult children allowing them the opportunity to live as independently as possible, especially if their prior involvement was more than typical for their culture.

The diagnostic criteria presented earlier in this book provide professionals with guidelines for determining AS. A practical list of specific behaviors known to impact the social skills of teens and adults with AS is more useful. The specific behaviors of AS known to interfere with social relationships for teens and adults include:

- awkward use of language, despite strong vocabulary and grammar

- poor understanding and social use of language

- difficulty interpreting and using nonverbal communication

- difficulty understanding the perspectives of others

- difficulty interpreting figurative language

- a perceived lack of empathy for others

- a preference for predictability and sameness

- a tendency to have attention and organizational difficulties, despite average to above-average intellect

- a tendency towards specific and intense interests

- difficulty integrating sensory information

- motor clumsiness or awkwardness

- problems regulating anxiety and mood.

Awkward use of language

An individual with AS often has various language skills that range from delayed to advanced. The wise range of language capabilities is sometimes referred to as peaks and valleys. Peaks and valleys in language skills can be misleading to others and are often highly problematic for the person with AS. The peaks generally involve strong expressive vocabulary; good speech articulation; and strong sentence structure. The valleys typically involve poor understanding and social use of language.

For listeners it is easy to assume that a person who has a strong, expressive vocabulary, and good use of grammar will also use the language well to communicate and interact with others. This assumption is based on the fact that most development, including the development of language skills, occurs in an even and uniform fashion. While everyone has strengths and weaknesses, the peaks and valleys in language development for teens and adults with AS are generally greater than those seen in the typical population. This occurs because the good skills are very good and the weak skills are very weak, causing the difference to be greater than that seen in a typical population. It is the difference that causes confusion for the listeners as they attempt to interpret the perspective of the speaker.

George agreed to co-present with me on the topic of accommodating the needs of employees with autism spectrum disorders in the workplace. We decided to start the presentation by providing our colleagues with an overview of the diagnostic criteria for autism and Asperger Syndrome. I would present the background information on the diagnostic criteria and George would present the helpful accommodations. To be prepared we got together to practice the presentation. When I got to the part of the presentation on the peaks and valleys in language development and used the term "pedantic," George asked me to clarify exactly what I meant by the term. I said, "A person who presents knowledge in a formal or precise way." He responded, "Oh, I get it. A 970,000 pound fully loaded Boeing 747 lifts off the ground because of the simple principle that as incompressible fluid increases in fluid velocity, it results in a simultaneous decrease across the fluid." The reality is that George understands AS all too well as he responds with a pedantic statement. He is brilliant in his

field of aeronautical engineering, yet needs accommodations in the workplace to perform to his potential. He
knows the definition of the word "pedantic," as he does
for most words, but he doesn't understand how that term
applies to the diagnostic criteria for AS, because how
could being pedantic be a "bad" thing?

Social use of language

Pragmatics is the set of rules that governs the social use of language.
Social rules are generally unwritten and unstated, complex, con-
stantly changing, and affect most areas of social interaction. These
include, but are not limited to, proximity to others when talking; nonverbal communication; greetings and farewells; conversation; the
speech act; effective listening; and the roles of speaker and listener as
they pertain to gender, age, and status. Violations of pragmatics are
fairly easy to identify by people who do not have AS, and lead to
frequent misunderstandings.

It is important to understand that the violations in pragmatics
occur for a variety of reasons. The person with a social pragmatic difficulty may not understand the purpose of many of the social rules of
language use and for this reason may not choose to adhere to the rules
as tightly as other people might. He may be able to memorize and
even apply a rule, but it doesn't seem natural so the rule is less rigidly
applied. It is sometimes a matter of really believing that this requirement is essential for quality interactions. This is especially true for
greetings and farewells. Since he may not need or require others to
use greetings and farewells it can be hard to really know and believe
that other people have this need. This is not uncommon since we all
view the world and our relationships through our own lens which is
molded from our own personal experiences. If it is my experience not
to need greetings and farewells when someone enters or exits a room
I may struggle to understand and believe that this is a strong requirement for others. It makes perfect sense that I may not completely

embrace this need of others, thinking that it is silly or even ridiculous to require certain social behaviors.

The person with social pragmatic problems may struggle with the speech act including sentence formation, word choice, sound articulation, and paralinguistic features. This struggle may provoke anxiety alone, yet when paired with social interactions with others causes extreme anxiety. This combination of expressive language difficulties, social challenges, and anxiety can lead to considerable pragmatic problems in initiating a conversation, topic maintenance, and adhering to a topic of mutual interest. In this case there are just too many variables to manage to allow the social interaction to be smooth and gratifying for the speaker and listener and the person with AS needs support from the communication partner to move beyond this place.

Pragmatic difficulties can improve when both speaker and listener understand the underlying nature of the social pragmatic problems. The problems are not presented to confuse the communication partner or to declare oneself as a completely self-absorbed and egocentric person, but as a result of underlying social pragmatic misunderstanding. This is the area in which neurotypicals (NTs) must increase their understanding of the person with AS in order for real progress to occur. Those with typical social pragmatic skills must learn to take the perspective of the person with social pragmatic difficulties and begin to *think in autism*. It is at this point that NTs can compromise and extend understanding to the person who is struggling rather than discounting the conversation and avoiding the person. Acceptance, compromise, and understanding are the supportive features that will allow teens and adults with AS the freedom to practice and apply social skills that are required to increase social competence.

Teenagers and adults with AS need others to understand the struggle and provide support where appropriate. The following sections address the specific types of pragmatic problems experienced by many teens and adults with AS. This information can be used by a teen or adult with social pragmatic difficulties as a way to expand his or her understanding of how NTs view certain pragmatic behaviors and can also serve as a training ground for NTs who need to increase their understanding of social pragmatic difficulties.

Pragmatics: Greetings and farewells

A person with AS may neglect to use any form of greeting when entering or exiting a room or may say "hello" and then pause for what appears to be an eternity because he doesn't know how to move forward in the conversation. When exiting a room he may say "goodbye" and then stay until the wait-time becomes so awkward that everyone begins to wonder what is happening; conversely, he may exit the room without saying anything, an act that also prompts people to wonder what has happened. This can apply to all forms of communication including letters and especially e-mails.

> One of my students never uses a salutation, closing, or signature on an e-mail. It is sometimes unnerving to get an e-mail without a salutation because I am not sure that it is intended for me and, when there is no closing or signature, I can only identify who wrote the e-mail by the return address. Sometimes it is not possible to figure out the sender because the college e-mail system uses codes and not actual names. I am sure that he is not aware of the stress this causes me, as the listener, when he neglects to use a proper greeting or signature. I do identify it as odd and would be upset if I didn't know that he has AS.

Pragmatics: Initiating a conversation

When initiating a conversation a teen or adult may begin by using what appears to the listener to be an irrelevant comment, by asking a question that appears to be off-topic or by asking a question that doesn't provide enough information for the listener to judge how to respond. This can be frustrating for the listener who may want the communication to go well, but needs more specific cues to know how to respond.

> I was driving Jenny to school the other day and she scared me to death. Before the car came to a complete stop she opened the door, jumped out and yelled to a classmate, "What did you think about that game yesterday?" The boy yelled back, "What are you talking about?" Jenny replied, "The game?" It was obvious that he had no idea what she was talking about and she did not seem to pick up the cue that he needed more information to understand her question. He was far enough up the sidewalk to just walk away, and it was pretty clear to me that he did not want to have a conversation. I had a feeling that this had happened before. Jenny doesn't understand the perspectives of others and struggles to interpret nonverbal communication. She really did not comprehend that this boy did not understand her question and that he had attempted to cue her to this fact. She was oblivious to the subtle verbal cues for more information and even his nonverbal communication that the conversation was just not worth the effort.

Pragmatics: Maintaining a conversation of mutual interest

A person who struggles to maintain a conversation of mutual interest may inadvertently direct the conversation towards a topic of his or her own special interest. The teen or adult who uses this conversation strategy may do so because the special interest is a topic in which he or she has extensive knowledge, experience, a strong personal interest and confidence in discussing. It makes perfect sense that when approaching an uncomfortable situation, like a conversation, a teen or adult may guide the conversation in a direction of comfort and familiarity.

Unfortunately this strategy can lead to misunderstandings and be viewed by the listener as a type of "hijacking" of the conversation. This strategy can annoy a listener and impede future conversations.

> I hadn't seen Nick for a long time so when we bumped into each other at the mall it was fun to try to catch up. The mall is within walking distance of his home so he frequently goes there to hang-out and spend time. I asked him about his parents and his siblings. He answered all of my questions with a quick "yes" or "no"; then I paused. This was his chance to tell me everything about his new special project. He had built a satellite dish that has the power to pick up sounds from space and he had hooked it to his computer to monitor the sounds. He knew everything about this kind of project including the fact that one of the co-founders of a major software company had just donated millions of dollars to a similar project. I found the conversation interesting, but it really wasn't what I wanted to talk about. I really wanted to know how he was doing, but I just had to guess that he was all right because he was so happy with his project.

Pragmatics: Changing topics abruptly

Changing topics in the middle of the conversation without providing a clear transition can be problematic for the listener. Teens and adults with AS may struggle to maintain a topic of conversation for more than a few reciprocal back-and-forth cycles between the speaker and the listener, resulting in a need to change the topic abruptly so that they can maintain the conversation. The problem with changing the topic in the middle of a conversation is that the listener will struggle to understand how to participate in the conversation. The speaker needs to provide the listener with some type of transition warning before abruptly changing a topic.

> Ralph is a co-worker of mine. He is an unusual guy. We were talking the other day and I felt like I was riding a roller coaster. We started out talking about the project we are working on and then, all of a sudden, he was talking about a woman. I was feeling pretty stupid that I had no idea who he was talking about. It sounded like our boss was seeing a woman on the side, maybe during his lunch break or something. I couldn't figure out how Ralph knew about this, and it was one of those topics that I just wasn't comfortable asking him to clarify. I just let him talk until he was finished and said that I had to get back to work. It was really strange. I found out later that he was talking about a movie he wanted to see and it had something to do with a woman. At some point our conversation changed from our project to the movie, but I didn't get it and was too uncomfortable to ask. It is hard to talk to Ralph for more than a minute or two because he talks fast and he talks all over the place.

An example of a transition statement for Ralph might have been, "Could I change the subject for a minute to tell you about a movie I want to see?" When asked nicely it is very hard for other people to say "no."

Pragmatics: The speech act

Speech patterns in all languages provide information to the listener that goes beyond the words and is used to strengthen the clarity of the message. Many teens and adults with AS use a speech pattern that is either monotone or irregular. A monotone speech pattern is one in which a speaker uses a single unvaried pitch, rhythm, stress, and intonation. Every sound, syllable, and word has the same emphasis.

An irregular pattern on the other hand occurs when the speaker uses irregular patterns of rising and falling speech in the areas of pitch, rhythm, stress, and intonation. The irregular pattern confuses the listener who would generally depend upon standard speech patterns used in their language to gain a better understanding of the message. Speech patterns convey meaning and are called "paralinguistic" features because they provide "para" (or support) for "linguistics" (the parts of language).

In monotone and irregular speech patterns comprehension is diminished since the speaker is not providing adequate information for the listener. This leaves the listener with full responsibility for interpreting the message which interferes with the listener's ability to accurately interpret the statement made by the speaker. This can be frustrating to listeners and can repel them from future conversations.

Jimmy is a middle school student in one of my classes who is diagnosed with AS. He is one of my best students and he seems to like participating in class when he is interested in the topic we are discussing. Other than appearing to be shy, he has no other problems in class except that his speech is difficult to understand. It took me a while to figure out the exact problem with his speech: he raises his voice at the end of every sentence as if he were asking a question. At the beginning of last school year I asked everyone to tell the class how they planned to spend a long weekend. Jimmy said, "I will spend most of the weekend playing Play Station?" I wondered at the time if this meant that he was hoping to get a Play Station to play with or wanting someone from the class to invite him over to play their Play Station. It was confusing to know exactly what he meant by phrasing the statement in the form of a question. I know now that this is just his speech pattern. Understanding his speech has gotten easier over time, but I can see how this would be really distracting to people who do not know him well. He was aware of this problem and had taken speech therapy, but it still exists.

Nonverbal communication

Teens and adults with AS generally have significant problems interpreting nonverbal cues of others such as eye contact, facial expressions, body postures, and gestures. People who struggle to accurately interpret nonverbal communication are open to constant misunderstandings with others, including people who usually understand them and the nature of their struggles. With nonverbal communication accounting for as much as 55 percent of the meaning in face to face communication, difficulties in this area can significantly impede social interactions.

We were saying our goodbyes after a nice visit with my mother. We were in the driveway and my mother reached over to hug our middle son goodbye. She must have had a sad look on her face because she was sorry that we had to leave, but we had to get home to school and work. My son stepped back from her hug and in a stern voice said, "What did I do? I didn't do anything!" We were all surprised because we had all witnessed the interaction and knew that his grandmother was sad that we were leaving. Our son had interpreted his grandmother's sad expression as one of anger and he thought that the anger was directed at him. Everyone was upset now, not about leaving, but at Daniel for hurting his grandmother's feelings. All of his brothers yelled at him and called him a few choice names. He got even more upset and was yelling "Everyone hates me." After a couple of minutes we all calmed down. My mother realized almost immediately that Daniel's behavior was based on his misinterpretation of her expression and she was able to compose herself. Even after years of knowing that these things can and do happen, our initial response was still one of shock and anger.

Perspective-taking

For the teen or adult with AS the weakness or inability to take the perspective of another person and see that situation from his point of view can cause major misunderstandings that lead to considerable social problems. It is hard to say to what degree perspective-taking negatively affects social relationships of teens and adults with AS because the research varies, but most agree that perspective-taking is a problem.

Major researchers have hypothesized that impairment in perspective-taking is a core deficit of autism (Baron-Cohen 1989). However, this is not necessarily true with AS. In Hans Asperger's original description of his patients he commented on the good perspective-taking abilities of his subjects; he is quoted in his summary of the disorder stating that there was "an ability to engage in a particular kind of introspection and to be a judge of character" (Asperger 1991, p.73). Others suggest that individuals with AS may struggle in the area of perspective-taking, yet demonstrate better performance on perspective-taking tasks than do people with autism (Klin *et al.* 2000).

It does appear that many, if not all, teens and adults with AS struggle to some degree with perspective-taking. The good news is that, while these capabilities do not appear to develop intuitively, many teens and adults respond positively to direct instruction in this area.

In the book *Thinking About You Thinking About Me* (2007) Michelle Garcia Winner outlines the requirements for perspective-taking that are essential for social awareness and competency.

- Recognize the thoughtful presence of another person.

- Recognize the individuality of another person.

- Recognize that another person has his or her own personal set of emotions.

- Recognize and respond to the fact that another person has his or her own set of desires and motives.

- Recognize that another person has his or her own personality.

- Have an intuitive desire to learn about others' interests and personal histories.

- Develop and use memory of a person to facilitate and sustain interpersonal relationships, as well as create a base of understanding of that person's potential actions.

- Formulate language to inquire about another person.

- Understand social conventions surrounding specific environments.

- Understand social conventions specific to social contexts.

- Stay aware, through eye contact, of the shifting internal states of the communication partner. (p.27)

Social interactions can be significantly inhibited by poor perspective-taking, especially in conversations. Both the speaker and listener in any conversation must be able to attend to the perspective of the other person in order for a conversation to flow smoothly. Perspective-taking is also important in the event that there is a problem in the conversation, because perspective-taking allows the speaker or listener to identify a miscommunication so that he can repair the conversation by applying a fix-up strategy.

I was attending my daughter's soccer game and, although she is diagnosed with pervasive developmental disorder, one of the milder forms of an autism spectrum disorder, she does struggle considerably with perspective-taking. At half-time in the game she came over to me and I whispered a comment to her that I thought was funny at the time, but realized later was rather inappropriate. I commented on how fat some of the players were on the other team. My daughter laughed thinking that this was hysterical. I thought it was pretty funny at the time, but soon realized that it was a huge mistake. She immediately ran towards her teammate and friend yelling, "Guess what my dad just said?" My heart almost stopped because the friend was at least as large if not larger than any of the players on the other team. I yelled for her to stop and come back. I am so glad that she did because it could have been a terrible hurt for her friend. She didn't even think about how her friend might feel about that comment; of course, my thoughtlessness wasn't much help either.

Literal interpretation of language

Language is used to send and receive messages that are literal and fig-urative. Literal messages contain words that are used and interpreted exactly as they are defined in the dictionary. Figurative messages contain words that imply a meaning other than the literal interpreta-tion. Figurative language is used to create emphasis, amplify meaning, draw a comparison or contrast, or make a rhetorical point (Sutcliffe 2004). Examples of figurative messages include similes, metaphors, puns, parables, paradoxes, ironies, idiom, the use of onomatopoeia, and sarcasm.

An idiom is a word or phase that has a specific assigned meaning that can not be determined by the actual words themselves. Examples of idioms include "hit the books," which means to study the content in a book, not to physically strike a stack of books, "break a leg!", which means good luck, "grab a bite," which means to get something to eat, and "a quick study" refers to someone who learns new things rapidly. A simile is a comparison made between two dissimilar objects using "like" or "as." Examples of simile include, "his feet are as big as boats" or "she is as light as a feather." A metaphor states that one thing is like something else for example "he knew that he was toast when he got home," which means that he knew he was in trouble, or "this is a recipe for disaster," which means that all of the ingredients are present that could lead to a major problem.

Understanding figurative speech requires the ability to identify subtle relationships between words and phrases, derive meaning from a message based on prior experience rather than direct observation, and the ability to take the perspective of the speaker. Sarcasm especially requires the listener to know the speaker well enough to be able to determine whether his message is reliable or a joke.

Interpreting figurative speech is difficult for many teens and adults with AS. Misunderstandings occur when figurative speech is interpreted from a literal standpoint.

> My inability to speak "human" has impacted my ability to work well on a team. At seven years old, I was excited to play in my first school soccer game. My coach dragged me to the center of the field, and announced that I was going to play this position called "center forward." I had no idea what the position required, so I asked, "What am I supposed to do?" My coach yelled back, saying, "Just stay right there!" So I did. The referee blows the whistle, the game starts, I kick the ball, and I stay right there. I stay in the middle of field as the game unfolds all around me, as the opposing team starts to kick a goal. I stay there thinking about the pointlessness and stupidity of this center forward position. Should my coach want me to play this position again, I will refuse. I stay there even as my teammates yell, "Are you stuck?" I stay there, a little confused and frustrated at this point, even as my coach yells, " What are you doing?! Get in the game!" Then, I am confused in trying to obey my coach's two commands—how can I "stand right there," and "get in the game"? Finally, the game ends, my team is slaugh-

tered, and I'm irritated. My parents ask me, concerned, "What were you doing? Why weren't you playing?" I responded, very frustrated at this point, "I was playing! I was doing exactly what my coach said!" Since I couldn't understand any of my coach's nonverbal communication, I took his words literally. As you can imagine, taking only someone's words from a message leads to confusion and frustration.

Kati

Empathy

One of the greatest areas of misunderstanding related to AS is that of empathy. Empathy refers to the ability to identify with the feelings, thoughts, or attitudes of another person. It is the ability to feel sad when others are hurting and fearful when others are scared.

It is common for people who do not understand AS to observe the behavior and social mistakes of a person with AS, and assume that they do not have the capacity to identify with the feelings, thoughts, or attitudes of others, but this is just not true. People with AS can feel deeply about many things including those things that affect other people. Problems generally occur when the person with AS does not observe the hurt or concern in another person but, when the feeling is discovered, empathy follows. Sometimes teens or adults will need a little extra time to process the communication and some added clarity to the message or additional time to formulate a response. At other times they will require understanding when they respond to an emotional situation with what may appear to be a lack of sensitivity because empathy is not an all-or-nothing proposition.

The other day I was reading a newspaper article on a tragic highway accident that caused the deaths of seven high school athletes returning home from a game. I made a comment out loud that I was reading a very sad story. My teenage daughter came over and read a small portion of the article over my shoulder. Without hesitation she said, "I wonder if they won their game." At first I couldn't believe what I was hearing. I struggled to process that comment even though I know that she has AS and that competition is one of her pervasive interests. My first response was one of anger. I was thinking, How could you say such a thing? Who cares about whether they won or lost; that's not the point. I knew not to say anything at the time because she does care deeply about other people. This is just how she responds sometimes. I extended grace to her for this comment, but I do not think that others would be able to deal with what appears on the surface to be a heartless attitude.

Predictability and sameness

The need for predictability and sameness can be an asset and at the same time it can be a liability for the teen and adult with AS. As an asset the need for predictability and sameness can lead a person to become a model student or employee. The desire for sameness is often translated into rules and routines that assist a person in becoming regimented, orderly, faithful, consistent, loyal, and committed which are all positive attributes for friends, students, employees, and citizens.

As a liability, the strong need for predictability and sameness, when interrupted, can be quite stressful for the individual, leading to potential disruptions in relationships with friends, classmates, teachers, employers and the community.

I have always had a high need for predictability. I think that it comes from the anxiety I feel in virtually all situations. It seems that routine and order are the only things that give me peace. As a kid I really freaked out over change, but I have made a lot of improvement in that area. Today I would say that I like sameness and routine, but I won't die if something changes. I try to keep my

schedule pretty basic, but things happen. Overall I have
a pretty happy life, I just worry a lot.

Attention and organization

The struggle in paying attention and being organized are difficulties
experienced by many teens and adults with AS. Some struggle with a
short attention span that interferes with paying attention to anything
for more than a short period of time. Others struggle with a height-
ened attention that causes them to pay attention to everything.
Others find that they are highly distracted by sensory stimuli in the
environment and yet others are distracted by internal thoughts.
Hyperactivity sometimes accompanies attention problems. This can
be problematic for other people.

Many teens and adults report that, prior to receiving the diagnosis of AS, they were first diagnosed with Attention Deficit Disorder
(ADD) or Attention Deficit Hyperactivity Disorder (ADHD). This
seems to occur for two reasons: the behaviors are easier to observe,
and many physicians are more familiar and comfortable with this
treatable diagnosis. There are those who have both AS and ADD or
ADHD, but this is not the case for everyone.

Difficulties in paying attention will cause social problems.
Attending to a communication partner is essential for clear communication. When people struggle to pay attention during a conversation
they are more apt to interrupt, talk over others, change the topic
abruptly, misunderstand the communication, or be misunderstood.

Clear communication requires that the speaker and listener be
fully engaged in the exchange. Full engagement requires that the
attention goes beyond the correct physical posture to hearing and
processing each word along with an analysis of each motive of
the communication partner. Poor attending can lead to
miscommunication and to a general disorganization in every area of
life. This leads to problems keeping appointments, being on time,
missing job interviews, making deadlines, and missing birthdays. It
can also transfer to disorganized spaces (desks, rooms) which lead a

person to spend an inordinate amount of time searching for missing things or not having what is needed when it is needed. Being disorganized can be stressful.

> Homework is a terrible thing. I try to do it, but stupid things get in my way. I have always hated homework because I think that students should do school work at school and fun things at home. I started doing my homework to get everyone off my back. It took me four years to really "get it" that I had to write down every assignment every day to be sure that I knew what homework to do. I can't even begin to tell you how frustrating it is to spend a huge amount of energy every day to write down my assignments, to feel a little proud of myself and then to get home to find out that I do not have a textbook I need. This happens all of the time, but it is always something different. I just can't win. I hate homework!

Specific and intense interests

Enthusiastic preoccupation with unusual interests or excessive interest in common topics or objects is a trait experienced by most people with AS. Special interests may include topics such as reciting sports statistics, or having an unusually strong fixation on a particular subject, such as the weather. In many cases, these topics may be unusual, such as excessive interest in aliens, birthdates, automobile license plates, or bus routes. Some people change interests frequently while others may hold to one interest for many years.

Strong interests have advantages and disadvantages. The advantages of having strong special interests are that they can provide enjoyment, provide for recreation and leisure time, ensure greater predictability in life, facilitate conversations, lead a person to become an expert in a particular area, and many times lead to a successful vocation. The disadvantage of special interests is that they can consume an enormous amount of time that can interfere with the time needed to learn other skills and capabilities, including those necessary for building social relationships and life skills required for independent living.

> From the time I was ten years old I have been fascinated with meteorology. I used to spend every waking minute reading, studying or charting some topic related to meteorology. When I was eleven years old I began keeping charts and logs of our local weather, including the accuracy rates of our local weathercasters. To tell you the truth they weren't very accurate. I began making my own weather predictions and my accuracy rate was much higher. I was actually correct in my predictions approximately 62.5 percent of the time which is about 20 percent better than the best forecaster in our area. My high school science teacher helped me start a meteorology club at school that got me "hanging out" with other teenagers who were interested in weather. Other kids at school thought that it was pretty cool that I could predict the weather with accuracy so they let me report predictions each morning on the school radio station. Of course some kids still used this against me. I ended up going to college and majored in meteorology. It was difficult living at college so I ended up living at home and finishing my bachelor's degree on-line. It is okay because now I work part-time for our local weather service. I would like to work full-time, but right now I will take what I can get.

Difficulty integrating sensory information

Many teens and adults with AS have unusual reactions to sensory stimuli and struggle to regulate sensory information. Problems can occur in the areas of sound, light, touch, texture, taste, smell, pain, movement, temperature, and other stimuli. These unusual reactions may range from atypical underreactions to a sensation to severe overreactions. It is believed that the central nervous system may not accurately interpret sensory information, causing a reaction that is either under or over that observed in those who do not have AS. Integration and responses to sensory information can improve with carefully designed therapy. Many teens and adults report an improved capacity to cope with sensory difficulties as they age. Some people report that this improvement comes from the ability to cope better in general. Others report that as adults they now have more control over their environment and can either change or avoid situations that are bothersome. Yet others report the discovery of medications that take the edge off their sensory struggles.

> When Gary was little I had to watch him very carefully. He was clumsy and was always falling down or bumping into things. He would hurt himself pretty good sometimes, but hardly ever cried. I became very concerned about his response to pain when he was ten. He fell off his bike cutting his knee so badly that he needed stitches. The problem was that I didn't know he hurt himself until about an hour after it happened. The injury did not bother him enough to come in to get help. He finally came into the house because the blood on his sock was bothering him. He wasn't upset about his knee, but he couldn't stand having anything on his sock. I really do not understand why he would be bothered by the sock and not the injured knee, but in this area he has always been an enigma. He still only wears cotton pants and shirts and he is 35 years old.

Reactions to sensory stimuli can range from mild to severe. Of course, the stronger the reaction the more likely the stimuli is to interfere with a person's life. The interference is usually caused when the person restricts activities so that he is not bombarded by unpleasant sensory experiences. In the event that unpleasant experiences do occur, whatever is happening at the time can be affected.

If a person has a strong sensitivity to certain scents she may not be able to go into new restaurants or certain areas of town, ride on a crowded bus or subway, or be in groups of people who might wear perfumes or colognes. Her food choices may be restricted, since smell and taste are closely connected. Restrictions in food will invariably narrow social choices and opportunities since so many of the world's cultures socialize around food, as in sharing meals together. She may not be able to go into loud places or crowded settings. This could inhibit attending concerts, going to shopping malls, amusement parks, or riding on a freeway.

Aversive responses to the senses can be stressful, anxiety-producing, painful, and exhausting.

Motor clumsiness

The physical difficulties experienced by many people with AS include motor awkwardness such as walking with an unusual gait or general clumsiness. There can also be fine motor difficulties that affect the quality and speed of motor planning required for handwriting and other fine motor tasks.

Posture and movement are forms of communication. When a person moves in a way that is not typical, others notice. The interests and desires of a person with AS might not be inhibited by his unique physical characteristics, but the stereotypes and prejudices of others that appear when someone looks different are real and do inhibit a person's chances of getting ahead.

> In primary school I used to hate recess because everyone would play some kind of sport and I just wanted to run around, swing or read a book. I have never been athletic. My family is into eating well and staying active, but I don't think that you would say that any of us are

athletic. My dad was a Boy Scout leader for years so I joined his troop when I was eight. I really did not like the camp outs and I never fit in with the other kids, but I did like hiking. Since I was a kid I have hiked. When I got older I noticed on a few long hikes that many of the trails in my area needed markers and shelters, so for a scout project I designed and built two shelters on a heavily hiked trail. I also marked the trail and prepared an information guide so that people would know all about the trail. While I wasn't very coordinated as a kid and actually I am still not very coordinated, I am healthy. I enjoy hiking as my hobby and hope that I can hike forever.

To summarize the experiences of teens and adults with AS, it is fair to say that AS is a disability of misunderstanding. It makes perfect sense that chronic, yet unpredictable, misunderstandings would cause any teen or adult with AS to view the social world as impossible to navigate. It is the unpredictability that is a significant cause of constant anxiety in the lives of many people with AS. For this reason many choose to self-segregate to avoid the hassles and pain.

Temple Grandin (1999) states that the single most prevalent feeling present in the life of an adult with autism is "anxiety." It is understandable that any person with social and communication difficulties would respond with anxiety to a social world that requires such highly developed social capabilities, yet in so many instances the rules are unwritten and ever-changing.

While the situation seems impossible, it is not. We have already learned that social progress can be made by teens and adults, and that social progress has the potential to bring about positive consequences. It is now time to see that some of the deficits listed can be reframed as assets (Bolick 2001).

The individual with AS is innately free from many of the social instincts that keep so many people bound by convention. This freedom allows the person to think outside of the box, leading potentially to creative solutions to many complex problems. Professor Simon Cohen-Baron performed a posthumous examination of two famous physicists, Sir Isaac Newton and Albert Einstein. Newton is credited with discovering the laws of gravity while Einstein developed the theory of relativity. Cohen-Baron's examination revealed that each displayed many characteristics common to AS (Derbyshire 2003). While Cohen-Baron admits that it is impossible to make a proper diagnosis posthumously it is interesting to speculate that these physicists were unencumbered by convention, freeing them to make spectacular discoveries. It may also be Newton's and Einstein's strong interests that fueled their tireless pursuit of scientific discovery.

The preference of many with AS for predictability and sameness can lead a person to become a model student or employee due to their natural adherence to rules and expectations. The tendency towards sameness can lead a person to develop a strong sense of right and wrong. This sense of right and wrong can lead to a hearty sense of social justice and honesty. Social justice and honesty are two attributes that are greatly needed in every society.

To further understand the social predicament of teens and adults with AS, it is essential to understand the highly social world in which we live. The next section of the book covers social and communication requirements.

1   A Social World

WHAT ARE SOCIAL SKILLS?

Social skills are the capabilities that we are expected to use to interact with others in our society. They are based on the social norms of our society and they tell us what attitudes and behaviors are considered to be normal, acceptable and expected in a particular social situation.

For you and me social skills are important because they allow us to interact with each other with predictability, so that we can more readily understand each other and be understood. Without an agreed-upon social way of interacting, it is very hard to prevent misunderstandings. It is important for us to be able to interact with clarity.

It is also important to know that people who have well-developed social skills are generally viewed by others in their society as competent and successful. They also tend to be well liked by others, while those who struggle to master the social skills are often viewed by society as inept. Failure to learn adequate social skills can lead to isolation, feelings of loneliness, frustration, rejection, and poor self-esteem. For those with AS it is important to know that this failure is the result of your disability, not of your own doing or from the lack of teaching or effort.

For society social skills are important because they provide us with order, predictability and also transmit our society's morals, values, motives, social roles, language, and symbols from one generation to the next. All of these attributes and behaviors are considered by society as essential for survival.

Social skills consist of three basic elements: social intake, internal process, and social output. Social intake refers to our seeing and understanding the words, vocal inflection, body language, eye contact, posture, gestures, and other cultural behaviors accompanying a social message. Internal process refers to our interpretation of the social message in addition to recognizing and managing our own emotions and reactions. Social output refers to how we respond to the message through our own words, vocal inflection, body language, eye contact, posture, gestures, and cultural behaviors.

It is important to understand that social skills are learned behaviors. They are first taught within the family and then reinforced in the school and community. Social skills are taught through a variety of methods including setting rules or standards for acceptable behavior, modeling and observing the social behaviors of others, and the direct teaching of social skills. Using social skills teaches children how to respond in acceptable ways to difficult situations. Social skills are strengthened through support or reinforcement and diminished through ignoring or punishment.

If you are a teen or adult with AS or a support person it is important to know that these methods for teaching social skills work well for children and teens who are neurotypical; however they are not as effective for children and teens with AS. Neurotypical (NT) people learn through instruction, but also have an enormous capacity to learn by observing and interpreting the behaviors of others. NTs are able to do this because they are able to interpret the perspectives of others. Unfortunately this is not often true for the person with AS, whose struggles with perspective-taking can diminish the accuracy of an interpretation from an observation. Basic social skills need to be taught through direct instruction paired with more opportunities for practice over a longer period of time. Once a rudimentary base of social understanding is achieved through direct instruction an older teen or adult can benefit from a less direct, yet guided approach that incorporates skillful observation at the center.

The specific social skills that make up that base of social understanding include the following:

- the use of proper greetings and farewells

- taking turns

- being patient

- being polite and courteous

- being kind

- being respectful

- listening to others

- waiting your turn to speak

- praising others

- knowing what jokes to tell or not tell

- knowing what topics of conversation are appropriate for which audiences

- respecting personal space

- refraining from making negative comments about people

- refraining from calling other people names

- refraining from swearing and making obscene gestures

- using good manners.

This list of social skills is important and must be taught. The best strategy for teaching specific social skills is through direct instruction. Direct instruction paired with many opportunities for practice is more apt to lead to successful acquisition of these skills.

Most of the skills on this list are generally taught during child-hood and the early teen years, but some teens and adults may want or require a refresher. If that is the case the best place to start is by teaching the concept of each social skill and then supporting the teen or adult as they apply the skills to various situations. A concept is taught using the following steps:

Concept example: Praising others

1. Define the concept: praise is the act of expressing approval or admiration.

2. List the salient features: an act, an expression, approval, or admiration.

3. Provide positive examples:

   ○ You are a very nice person.

   ○ Your hair is beautiful.

   ○ I like how you told that story.

4. Provide negative examples:

   ○ You are a terrible teacher.

   ○ That is an ugly dress.

   ○ I am thinking that you are nice, but I don't feel like saying anything to you.

5. Provide a prototype, a best example of praising others.

   ○ You are a marvelous person and I think that you are the best.

6. Give the learner opportunities to sort and identify positive and negative examples of praising others.

7. Give opportunities to practice praising others in a role-play or scripted situation.

After teaching the concept of praise and practicing the skill in isolation it is time to generalize the skill to other settings. This is the time when observation and reflection can be introduced. During each practice opportunity, have the child or teen note down observations and follow the opportunity with a time of reflection. Repeat this process with every skill while encouraging observation, reflection, and analysis.

For older teens and adults the teaching of social skills differs from methods used with children. It differs because in most instances they already have a good understanding of the social rules, but struggle to apply these rules in authentic situations. For the teen or adult who must memorize each rule, this is especially difficult since this approach does not lend itself very well to unexpected change. Therefore, there is a greater risk of failure given the rapidly changing social rules in many communities.

Every generation attempts to modify the social norms of its time. This typically occurs during the teenage years when many take part in changing social expectations. My generation, for example, worked at getting the larger society to accept that wearing blue jeans can be appropriate in many social settings. That was considered socially inappropriate by our parents. Other generations have modified the social norms in other ways. These included the increased use of slang, social communication where age has less influence on how we address each other than in past generations, and the roles of male and female in social interactions.

We live in an age where social norms are changing at a rapid rate. It is virtually impossible for any one human being to know and master every social skill required for every setting. Dr Grandin asks, "Does this give us an excuse to put aside the effort it takes to function socially? No. It just means that our social learning never stops" (Grandin and Barron 2005, p.24).

Grandin and Barron (2005) propose the idea that instead of attempting to teach specific social skills for each separate situation that we consider teaching broad principles that are more apt to apply across age and social setting. They call these principles The Ten Unwritten Rules of Social Relationships and predict that knowledge of these ten rules will lead to increased social awareness. The rules are as follows:

1. Rules are Not Absolute. They are Situation-based and People-based.

2. Not Everything is Equally Important in the Grand Scheme of Things.

3. Everyone in the World Makes Mistakes. It Doesn't Have to Ruin Your Day.

4. Honesty is Different from Diplomacy.

5. Being Polite is Appropriate in Any Situation.

6. Not Everyone Who is Nice to Me is My Friend.

7. People Act Differently in Public than They Do in Private.

8. Know When You're Turning People Off.

9. "Fitting In" is Often Tied to Looking and Sounding like You Fit in.

10. People are Responsible for Their Own Behaviors. (p.119)

WHAT ARE COMMUNICATION SKILLS?

Communication skills are the set of capabilities that we use to exchange information, thoughts, attitudes, ideas and feelings clearly and accurately. It is through communication that we get the information we need to survive.

Communication is comprised of the words we use, how we say the words, and our nonverbal communication. The words we use come from our language, how we say the words is determined by the paralinguistic rules of our language, and nonverbal communication is made up of the wordless messages we send through our body language. Paralinguistic cues are used by the speaker to emphasize communication for the purpose of providing clarity for the listener.

Communication requires a speaker and a listener. It is the role of the speaker to send a clear and concise message. It is the role of the listener to receive and correctly interpret the message sent by the speaker. In order to become effective communicators, we must develop the skills required by both the speaker and the listener.

The speaker

Speaking is the act of sending messages to others through spoken language. The speaker is the person who sends the message to others. As the speaker we must be able to convey a clear and concise message. In order to do this we must have a good command of our language, the paralinguistic cues that support our spoken language, and knowledge of nonverbal communication. We must also be concerned that our message is heard and understood by the listener.

It is the responsibility of the speaker to construct the message so that it can be understood by the listener, even if some type of mediation is required. This means that the speaker must have the capacity to see the perspective of the listener and be able to address his point of view.

The listener

Listening is the key to receiving messages. The listener is the person responsible for receiving the message. Listening is a combination of hearing what another person says and psychological involvement with the person who is speaking (Windle and Warren 1999). Listening requires more than hearing words. It requires a desire to understand another human being, an attitude of respect and acceptance, and a willingness to try to see things from another person's point of view.

> Listening in dialogue is listening more to meaning than to words… In true listening, we reach behind the words, see through them, to find the person who is being revealed. Listening is a search to find the treasure of the true person as revealed verbally and nonverbally. There is the semantic problem, of course. The words bear a different connotation for you than they do for me. Consequently, I can never tell you what you said, but only what I heard. I will have to rephrase what you said, and check it out with you to make sure that what left your mind and heart arrived in my mind and heart intact and without distortion. (Powell 1990, p.140)

Listening requires a high level of concentration and energy. It demands that the listener set aside his or her own thoughts and agendas. True listening requires suspended judgment, careful evaluation, and overt approval; all are needed to understand another's frame of reference, emotions, and attitudes. Listening to understand is, indeed, a difficult task (Windle and Warren 1999).

The specific skills required for effective listening include giving full attention to the other person, observing the other person, and then thinking about what the other person is trying to communicate (Bolton 1979). Giving full attention to the speaker means that the listener must pay attention to both the verbal and nonverbal message. A good listener leans gently towards the speaker, faces the other person squarely, maintains an open posture with arms and legs uncrossed, maintains an appropriate distance between the listener and the speaker, and provides nonverbal feedback to the speaker with head nods and a positive facial expression (Bolton 1979).

Giving full attention to the speaker includes paying attention to the words and feelings expressed by the speaker, to the speaker's non-verbal communication and to the accompanying paralinguistic cues. It is through the words, nonverbal communication, and paralinguistic cues that ideas are developed about what the speaker is trying to communicate. The listener must attempt to take the perspective of the speaker and try to see the communication from the speaker's point of view.

Language

Our language is the socially shared and agreed upon system of communication made up of symbols that we use with other people to express and exchange ideas, thoughts, attitudes, facts, and feelings. Language is learned through modeling and practice.

To acquire a language we must develop the linguistic knowledge of the language; including the sounds, word meaning, grammar, and social use of the language. These skills typically develop over time from birth to approximately eight years of age when most of the sounds and structures of most languages are in place. Language continues to develop in complexity throughout life as new vocabulary and concepts are acquired.

Albert Mehrabian (1972) discovered that words account for 7 percent of all meaning in communication that involves feelings and attitudes, attributing up to 93 percent of meaning to other variables.

Paralinguistic cues

Paralinguistic cues are the features of our speech that are used to emphasize communication for the purpose of providing clarity for the listener. These features include pitch, loudness, rhythm, stress, and intonation of the voice. Paralinguistic cues involve how something is said, not the content of what is said.

Pitch refers to the sound of the voice—high or low—and is measured on a Hertz scale. Loudness refers to the volume of the voice—loud or soft—and is measured in decibels. Rhythm refers to the metric pattern of the speech which differs within each language. Stress refers to the emphasis placed upon words in the communication that can change the intended message dependent upon which word is stressed. Paralinguistic cues increase the clarity of the intended message; therefore, they are essential for understanding and being understood by others.

To demonstrate the influence of paralinguistic cues on speech, let's examine the impact that stress places on the following sentence. If I say, "I didn't say you broke the window" and emphasize each word in the sentence differently, the implied meaning will change drastically with each statement. If I say, "*I* didn't say you broke the window," I am implying that, while I did not make the statement, someone else may have said that you broke the window. If I say, "I *didn't* say you broke the window," I am expressing some anger about the accusation that I am being accused of making the statement that you broke the window. If I say, "I didn't *say* you broke the window," I am implying that maybe I reported your breaking the window in some other way, like writing it down in a note or gesturing to someone that you broke the window. If I say, "I didn't say *you* broke the window," I am acknowledging that I did make a statement about a broken window, but did not say that you broke the window; maybe I said that someone else broke the window. If I say, "I didn't say you *broke* the window," maybe I actually said that you smashed the window or just cracked the glass. If I say, "I didn't say you broke the *window*," maybe I said that you broke something else, possibly the frame or the glass.

In each statement the underlying meaning is changed significantly as a result of the emphasis or stress placed on each word. If a seven-word sentence can possess six different meanings, as a result of changes in stress, one can imagine just how complicated language can be to interpret.

Intonation is the specific voice marker that communicates certain grammatical features within a language. In English an example of intonation as a grammatical feature would be the lowering of the voice at the end of a sentence when wanting to convey a statement. Others examples would include raising the voice at the end of a sentence to ask a question or expressing an abrupt, forceful utterance at the end of a sentence to make an exclamation.

Intonation is also used to express emotions such as joy, frustration, anger, and fear. When someone is startled in a fearful way, he might yell out the word "help" while strengthening the tone of his voice at the end of the word, making an exclamation along with increasing the loudness of the voice. This communicates to others that the person is making an urgent cry that someone should come to help. If someone feels embarrassed in a situation and wants to say something to recover her dignity, she might say the same word, "help," but raise the pitch of her voice while reducing the volume when saying the word. This will cause the listener to hear a shy or bashful person asking another for forgiveness with a slightly embarrassed tone.

Albert Mehrabian (1972) discovered that paralinguistic cues alone account for as much as 38 percent of all meaning in communication that involves feelings and attitudes. Paralinguistic cues and words together account for 45 percent of the meaning in communication that involves feelings and attitudes.

Nonverbal communication

Nonverbal communication is the process of communicating by sending and receiving wordless messages. These messages are sent through facial expressions, eye contact, gestures, body language, and posture.

Facial expressions result from the movements and positions of the muscles of the face. These movements convey to other people wordless messages related to the emotional state of the speaker. They are a primary source of conveying emotional information. A smiling face can convey pleasure or happiness while a frowning face conveys displeasure or sadness. The eyes are particularly expressive in conveying sadness, anger, frustration, confusion, and happiness.

Gestures are movements of the body that also convey wordless meaning. The meaning of a gesture is usually decided within a culture. For example in Germany a person holding up his thumb with his fingers folded back into a fist would be gesturing the number one as in the case of ordering one more beer in a pub, while in the United States holding the thumb up in the same gesture means "good job" or "I agree." If a person from the United States who was traveling in Germany held up his thumb with pleasure after ordering a round of beer for his group, he might find himself buying a second round when his wordless intent was to tell the waiter, "good job for the first round."

Posture also communicates wordless messages through the shape and position of the torso in relationship of the arms and legs. The arms placed tightly across the chest can communicate stubbornness, while arms that are open can communicate flexibility and trust. When people sit up and forward they communicate that they are interested in what others are saying; when they sit back they appear powerful and in control.

People communicate through nonverbal communication even when they might not want to communicate. The human body when awake will communicate even without permission.

Albert Mehrabian (1972) discovered that nonverbal communication accounts for 55 percent of all meaning when discussing feelings and attitudes. This means that of all three parts of the communication act—the words, the paralinguistic cues and the nonverbal communication—it is nonverbal communication that transmits the most meaning.

Mehrabian's findings are useful in explaining the importance of meaning, as distinct from words. This model is useful in illustrating the importance of factors other than words alone when trying to convey meaning (as the speaker) or to interpret meaning (as the listener). Care needs to be taken, however, in considering the context of the communication, since Mehrabian's study focused primarily on spoken communication of feelings and attitudes. Therefore his results should not be generalized to include all types of communication. However, it is essential to know that meaningful communication is comprised of words, paralinguistic cues, and nonverbal communication.

In order to communicate effectively a person must be able to listen as well as speak, but that is not the end of the story. A person can have the most highly developed language, but unless he or she is able to apply that language to social settings, the effectiveness will be impeded.

HOW ARE SOCIAL SKILLS AND COMMUNICATIONS RELATED?

Social and communication skills are related through pragmatics. Pragmatics in any language sets forth the standards or rules for the social use of the language. It is only when the speaker and listener both have command of these rules that clear, effective and meaningful communication can occur. Pragmatics is "the use of language to express one's intentions and to get things done in the world" (Gleason 2001, p.24).

Pragmatics includes the rules for conversation and the communication act. Rules of conversation include turn-taking, levels of formality, and topic maintenance. The communication act includes the appropriate rate of speech, pitch, stress, intonation, loudness, quantity of information, quality of information, and the directness of the information.

When pragmatics rules are violated it is easy to recognize that something is wrong. The good news is that pragmatics also governs the rules that determine how conversations are repaired—the "fix-up" strategies.

It is comforting to think that social skills are easy to learn and readily available to everyone, but this is just not true, especially for teenagers and adults with AS. AS is a disability that negatively affects the acquisition and appropriate use of social skills including the social use of language, but the situation is not hopeless. Social skills can be learned by teenagers and adults with AS when there is a desire combined with clear guidelines for making progress.

STEPS TO INCREASE SOCIAL COMPETENCE

Social awareness and competence will increase over time for the teen and adult with AS if she uses skillful observation, self-examination, analysis, implementation of personal strategies to address individual needs, and ongoing evaluation. The steps to increase social competence begin with an understanding of each part of the process and then move on to suggestions on how to get started.

Skillful observation is the action taken to recognize and note facts or occurrences in your social surroundings. Observation involves watching your social surroundings carefully and with great attention for the purpose of arriving at a judgment. A key to social progress is focusing predominantly on the people and interactions in your surroundings—observing words, behavior and attempting to see beneath the surface to the perspectives, meaning the point of view. It also includes observing the reactions of others and even examining your own reactions. Observations can be written down, charted, or stored in your memory. If you do not have a good memory or are inattentive, it is best to write down your observations.

One caution for the teen or adult with AS is developing observation skills that are accurate. Everyone views the world, including interactions between people from his or her own experiences. We all have lenses over our eyes, figuratively speaking, that influence how we interpret what we observe. Our lenses are greatly influenced by our abilities, life experiences, culture, and language.

Observing the social world is extremely difficult for the individual with AS for many reasons. Some experts think that there is a breakdown in social reasoning and judgment that negatively influences the accuracy of interpreting social behavior. For the teens or adults seeking to develop accurate observation skills another set of "eyes" may be required. This may involve enlisting another person who has well-formed observation skills to serve as your inter-rater. "Inter-rater" is a term used in the social sciences to describe the act of two people observing the same event at the same time, recording and then sharing their observations. The degree to which the two people concur on their observations is the degree consistency between the observations.

A test of inter-rater reliability would be following scenario: You and one other person decide to observe the number of times a parent in the park demonstrates a loving gesture toward his or her child. Loving gestures are hugs, pats, kisses, smiles, and affirming words. You watch the parent and child separately, for a predetermined amount of time, marking a tally every time you observe what you think is a loving gesture. At the end of the observation add the total number of loving gestures you observe and have the other observer add their total number of observations. Divide the smaller number by the larger number then multiply by 100 percent. If one observer marks three tallies during the time span and the other person records seven tallies, obviously the inter-rater reliability would be inconsistent.

3 divided by 7 = 0.42

0.42 multiplied by 100 percent = 42 percent

This will give you the percentage to which you agreed on the number of loving gestures. This is considered your "inter-rater reliability," the degree to which you are consistent in your observation. This calculation will not take into account error caused by chance, so any math wizards may choose to use Cohen's kappa coefficient which is a statistical measure of inter-rater reliability that measures the agreement between two raters taking into account the agreement that occurs by chance. If you want to determine the inter-rater liability when there are more than two raters you could use Fleiss' kappa coefficient.

Take time to talk about the observation. This type of practice, reflection, and discussion can stimulate strong observation skills in both raters.

Self-examination involves a reflective examination of your behavior including your thoughts, motives, and feelings. The behaviors to be examined are taken from the observations you make of yourself and your observations of others in your social surroundings. It is the combination of your observations and self-examination that will lead you to a better understanding of your social surroundings. These understandings can serve as the basis for identifying specific strategies that are most apt to meet your needs given the requirements of your community.

The implementation of personal strategies refers to the act of putting to use strategies that will meet your individual needs based upon your observations and self-examination; other factors, including personal preferences, interests, and availability of resources must also be considered. Personal strategies might include script writing and role-playing to prepare for social interactions; writing lists to prioritize and remember events; or using a notebook or personal digital assistant (PDA) to keep notes and records that might be needed in social interactions.

Ongoing evaluation is the step that allows you to evaluate the effectiveness of each strategy. It is also the point in which you may decide to revise your strategy and try again. Since social requirements are ever changing and social learning never ends, evaluation will be ongoing throughout your life as it is for everyone.

Now that you know the process towards increased social competence it is time to get started. The first step in changing or modifying any behavior is to accept that a change is needed. This can be the greatest challenge for anyone because change is hard. It is especially hard to face and admit that change is needed in an area that has caused significant problems or suffering in the past or in an area where you have attempted change before without success.

It is important to be willing to be honest with yourself. For those of you with AS it probably won't take too long to recognize and agree that social problems exist and that improvement is needed, since this is probably something that you have been hearing from others for most of your life. You may be accustomed to living with negative consequences such as unemployment, underemployment, overly dependent living, or isolation; but you would really like to benefit from the positive consequences of satisfying work, greater independence, and improved relationships with others.

In the event that you are still unsure you might want to think about your current situation and ask yourself the following questions.

- Am I having difficulties making or maintaining friendships?

- Do I feel that I am frequently misunderstood?

- Do I have trouble understanding the social behavior of others?

- Am I having social problems at school or work?

- Am I having trouble in a relationship as a result of social problems?

- Do I think that my social behaviors are inhibiting my success or progress in any area of life?

- Are my friends and family pestering me about my social skills?

If you have answered yes to any of these questions you probably could benefit from the information that helps increase social awareness and competence. If you continue to be unsure you can complete the "Personal Rating Scale" in My Journal on page 164. If you answer all of the sections at 75 percent or higher, you are probably already receiving positive consequences as a result of adequate or better social skills; if your scores in any area fall below 75 percent, you may choose to examine that area more carefully.

After determining that change would help, the next step is to begin observing your social patterns of interaction and the interactions of others. These can be noted in specifics or as general impressions. Observations should be made and noted concerning your effectiveness or lack of effectiveness.

The next step is to plan and practice your new social skills in various settings, from visits to the doctor's office to job interviews.

The last step is to assess and reflect upon your newly applied skills for the purpose of making changes if needed. Each of the following chapters provides a structured approach to practicing the steps to increased social competence.

Each chapter is divided into four sections entitled The Topic, The Challenge, The Explanation and The Solution. The section entitled The Topic includes clear definitions and descriptions of each term along with reasons people give for the importance of that area in life. The section entitled The Challenge presents authentic stories gathered from persons with AS for the purpose of demonstrating the concerns involved in each topic. The section entitled The Explanation includes the concerns stated by individuals with AS and their families in regards to each topic. The section entitled The Solution provides easy-to-follow, step-by-step guidelines for practicing the steps to increased social awareness and competence in areas described in the book.

2　　　Friends and Family

In this chapter the relationships between people are explored. The specific topics covered are acquaintances, family, friends, dating, marriage, parenting, and strangers. Each topic is defined and the purpose for each relationship is presented. Personal stories are told that describe the struggle and unique challenges that teens and adults with Asperger Syndrome experience in relationships along with an explanation for the struggle. Practical solutions to the challenges are then presented in an easy-to-follow, step-by-step format.

THE TOPIC: ACQUAINTANCES

Acquaintances are people with whom we share a casual connection. These connections usually come from some type of shared experience. Acquaintances include schoolmates, co-workers, bus drivers, service providers, teachers, professors, store clerks, neighbors, waiters, attendants, and parishioners.

Acquaintances are important because they make up the largest group of people with whom most of us have regular contact. Acquaintances occupy shared spaces and provide assistance with the tasks required for daily living. They also provide a large group of people in which possible friends may be discovered.

The degree of complexity in communication required by this type of relationship varies, but generally these relationships require simple forms of communication that may include greetings and farewells, simple requests, or friendly talk about the weather paired with non-verbal gestures like a smile, nod, a wave or an eye gaze. While the communication required for most acquaintances is simple other factors can cause acquaintance level relationships to become highly susceptible to miscommunication for teens and adults with AS.

The challenge

I moved into my own place right after finishing two years at a technical school majoring in computer programming. My parents and I decided that I would lease a flat in the city close to my new job. We selected a place located on the city bus line to make it easier for me to get from one place to another, especially to work. I am generally anxious when faced with new experiences. The thought of riding a city bus to work made my stomach feel a little sick. I had learned years earlier that I needed to plan for new experiences. The best way to plan for a bus ride would be to prepare a note to remind me to introduce myself to the driver and to tell him or her the office address. I had learned in the past that if I tell a driver where I want to go, he or she will usually get me to the closest bus stop. I decided to give the bus ride a practice run so that I would know exactly what to expect on my first day of work.

I wrote the list with the essential information and got on the bus. I introduced myself to Ken, the driver, and told him my work address. From that day forward I would get on the bus and tell Ken to "Take me to my office." This became a joke between us. I have always been a person who likes to joke around. Ken would just stop the bus at the stop closest to my office.

This worked great until one day when Ken suddenly took off work. I didn't know that he was going to be away so I got on the bus and I told the substitute bus driver to "Take me to my office." She asked me where I wanted to go and I said it again, "Take me to my office." She became very upset and just told me to go sit down, look out the window and if there was anything that looked like my office building to let her know. I did what I was told, but every building looked the same and I just couldn't remember my office address since I hadn't used it in such a long time. I didn't have the script with me that I used on the first bus ride. I ended up riding the bus for two hours. The bus driver eventually drove the entire route and took me back to the stop that I got on and yelled at me something about how much money I owed the city for my morning bus ride. Not only did I get into trouble on the bus, but I also got into trouble on my job because I did not call to tell them that I would be late.

Jonathan

The explanation

The largest group of people with whom we have regular contact is acquaintances. Acquaintances are highly variable and complicated from the standpoint that you never know how an acquaintance might respond to a person who has communication difficulties. Regular contact with acquaintances is essential for teens and adults who want to live independently.

In Jonathan's situation he was well prepared for his first bus ride in his new city. He successfully planned and introduced himself to the bus driver along with providing the exact location of his office. With this information the bus driver was able to assist in selecting the bus stop closest to Jonathan's office. This worked well and became an enjoyable interaction with the familiar bus driver. Jonathan began to depend upon the predictability of his bus ride routine. He was startled by the unexpected change in drivers and found himself unprepared. He did not have the address for his office in his belongings and he was unable to identify any other way to solve the problem. When faced with the unexpected he resorted to using a reliable and familiar communication pattern, "Take me to my office," but this did not provide the substitute bus driver with the information she needed to identify his bus stop. The bus driver interpreted his request as odd, so he was dismissed and the problem was not solved.

This type of miscommunication is all too familiar to teens and adults with AS. Communicating with an acquaintance can be highly susceptible to miscommunication even though the actual content of the exchange may be simple, as in the case of simple comments or questions, with fewer exchanges than those required for friends. The actual reason for this increased susceptibility can be found in the nature of the acquaintance relationship.

Acquaintances by definition are casual relationships, meaning that there is no strong sense of responsibility to watch out for the benefit of the other person. Acquaintances are neither friends nor family. They have not made a social commitment to understand the other person or even to get along. This can pose a threat to clarity in verbal exchanges. Even short conversations may become complicated when either the speaker or listener is not committed to extending the effort required to guarantee that communication is clear and that any miscommunication is corrected. This places a tremendous responsibility on the person with the need to communicate for the purpose of accessing information or services; she has to be sure that the communication is clear and successful.

This burden can be exasperating for the teen or adult with AS who will struggle to spontaneously interpret social idiosyncrasies of communication from an acquaintance and who may also struggle to identify that a communication problem has actually occurred.

When a miscommunication is identified, the teen or adult with AS may struggle to apply the correct "fix-up" strategy, those strategies used to correct misunderstandings in communication. In the event that he or she correctly identifies a miscommunication, the application of a "fix-up" strategy may still seem awkward in application and timing, bringing the same results—conflict related to miscommunication.

Being late for work one time may not jeopardize Jonathan's standing with his employer, but in reality situations like this occur in the life of teens and adults with AS with alarming, unpredictable regularity. It is the unpredictability that contributes greatly to the level of anxiety that many teens and adults must live with and it is the unpredictability that causes many to stop trying to navigate life outside of a very small circle.

The solution

In many instances the best solution for communicating with acquaintances is to prepare a script or a list that provides the exact information you will need for various types of communication. As for the bus ride, Jonathan was initially well prepared for his new experience. He knew he had to introduce himself to the driver and then provide the exact address of his office. Unfortunately, once he established a routine he neglected to carry the essential information needed in the event of a change.

Learning to interact with acquaintances can be as simple as observing those people in your life who fit into the category of acquaintance, thinking about that person's role in your life, and preparing an appropriate script that includes the essential information that will assist you in the interactions with each acquaintance.

The steps to more effective social interactions with acquaintances are:

1. List the names or titles of the people in your life whom you consider acquaintances. It is best to organize this information in a notebook or personal digital assistant (PDA); be sure to include people like classmates, teachers, co-workers, service providers, clerks, bank teller, and bus drivers.

2. Alphabetize the list so that you are able to access the information easily when needed.

3. List the essential role of each acquaintance.

4. List the essential information that you may need to communicate with each acquaintance. Be sure to use good note-taking principles. (See the note-taking guidelines in Chapter 6, Adaptive Tools.)

5. Observe the acquaintances on your list, write down what you see and think about each person's role in your life. For example the bank teller assists you in making withdrawals, deposits or transfers of money. Remember that it is important for the bank employee to be helpful and provide service to the bank's clients. You may observe that a teller is friendly and talks a lot. You may observe this person starting a greeting with a statement about the weather or inquiring about your well-being. This is called "small talk." You may observe other people in the line in front of you sharing short responses to the tellers "small talk." You may also observer that the teller asking, "How can I help you today?" So, when writing a script for the bank teller, you will need to prepare two parts, the first is having a way to respond to "small talk" and the second is how to make your specific banking request.

6. When making "small talk" it is important to know that many people select safe, predictable and impersonal topics when talking to acquaintances like short comments on the present condition of the weather, for instance, "It is really hot today." Many people ask questions about the other person's well-being, for instance, "How are you today?" This can be misleading since the person asking the question is in essence using this question as a greeting rather than an honest inquiry about the true well-being of the person. In almost every case the acquaintance would

respond to this type of inquiry with, "I'm good," or "I'm okay."

7.   Based on your observations write a short script of the social interaction in your notebook or PDA that you believe will lead to a positive interaction with each acquaintance. Remember to use language that is clear, concise and polite. Be sure to include the prompts to remind you to be expressive in your communication and body language.

8.   Rehearse and practice your scripts using your notebook or PDA. It would be best to preview your script prior to seeing an acquaintance, for example, if you are planning to grocery shop or visit the bank preview your scripts before going. For appointments with your doctor, dentist or mental health provider it might be best to refer to your notes at the appointment, if needed. You will want to select the practice and reminder that allows for the most smooth and natural interaction. Reading from a PDA in front of the grocery store clerk might inhibit that interaction; however, if it is needed to move forward in your interactions with others that is fine. It is better than not interacting.

9.   After using the scripts with each acquaintance be sure to take some personal time to write down your impressions about the effectiveness of the social interaction. Be sure to include comments on your behavior and the behavior of the acquaintance.

10. To simplify the analysis of the observation create a scale of 1 to 5 that you can use to rate the effectiveness of your social interaction, with 1 being poor and 5 being very good. You might choose to use the following questions to guide your self-assessment.

     ○ Was the communication clear between the acquaintance and myself?

- ○ Was the interaction with the acquaintance positive?

- ○ How do I know that the interaction was positive?

- ○ Was the purpose of the interaction accomplished?

- ○ Did I use the right words? How would I rate my paralinguistic cues? How would I rate my body language?

- ○ If the interaction was not successful, why?

11. After ranking your performance you may choose to revise the script.

12. Practice the revised script. If you have any difficulty identifying the exact problem with any acquaintance ask someone you trust for his appraisal of the situation. If you find his insight to be fair you may choose to incorporate the suggestions into a revised script.

13. Keep the notebook or personal daily planner with you. It is also highly recommended that you make a copy of the notebook or make a back-up copy for the PDA in the event that it is misplaced or lost.

Planning ahead by preparing a notebook or PDA with scripts can increase the effectiveness of social interactions with acquaintances, especially when unexpected situations arise. After a time of successful practice you will no longer need the script. The script is an external support that will eventually turn into an internal script for interacting with acquaintances.

THE TOPIC: FAMILY

The term "family" can refer to a number of different groupings of people, but in this book "family" refers to those people who form a social group consisting of parents or guardians, their children (whether living together or not), and persons closely related such as grandparents, uncles, aunts, and cousins.

Contemporary western society generally views the family as a place where intimacy, love, and trust are encouraged and where individuals may escape from the demands of a complicated world. Families provide love, protection, support, warmth, tenderness, understanding, and instruction.

While it is generally expected that the people in families will always love, trust, and understand each other, this is not always the case. Families are made up of people just like any other group. The fact that people are involved means that there are occasionally going to be problems. Many of the problems between people in families occur in the area of communication.

Communication can be difficult in all families, but especially difficult in families where one or more of the members have communication problems. The unique and pervasive difficulties in the area of communication for teens and adults with AS can be particularly stressful for them and for everyone in their family.

The challenge

When Brittney was born she was the most beautiful baby I had ever seen. Her facial features were perfect. In spite of her beauty she was a difficult and demanding baby. She cried frequently and was difficult to soothe. She struggled to adapt to new people and places. As a pre-schooler she struggled to get along with other children. She was viewed by other children and their parents as demanding and bossy. It was hard to get other children to agree to play with her for more than one play date, so most of her contact with other children took place at organized group activities like Sunday school and dance class.

Brittney has always had a high need for predictability. I discovered when she was very young that I had to tell her the next day's schedule before she went to bed each night. I also discovered that she would often anger others by her inability to understand their perspectives or even know when social problems were arising. I found it necessary to eavesdrop on her conversations with everyone so that I could intervene in the event that a communication problem arose. She seemed agreeable to my listening and was fairly open to my prompting her to interact better with others. This was true for everyone except her grandmother.

Visits with Brittney's grandmother were infrequent, but often enough that her grandmother felt comfortable taking on the role of teacher. We would visit her grandmother and, during the visit, Brittney's grandmother would try to teach her how to complete various tasks that she felt were lacking, like making her bed and picking up after herself. Rather than going along with the instruction she became resistant and defiant, which caused her grandmother to also become resistant. A vicious cycle ensued. At times their bantering became quite hurtful. Brittney knew at some level that her grandmother's instruction, while it was well-meaning on the surface, was actually an indictment of her immaturity. I tried to referee the exchanges, but couldn't get either one to understand the other.

Brittney was diagnosed with Asperger Syndrome which assisted our family, especially her grandmother, in understanding her developmental immaturity in addition to her inappropriate social communication with her grandmother and others. The diagnosis allowed the grandmother to overlook certain behaviors, recognizing that the best way to support her granddaughter's maturation was to be positive about the things she could do while encouraging her to try new things. She also began to understand that her development could not be rushed nor pushed.

Janice, Brittney's mother

P.S. Brittney is 15 years of age. Her parents thought from the time she was three years old that she had some type of mild autism spectrum disorder, but chose not to have her evaluated until she was 14. Even without a formal diagnosis the family provided the adaptations and supports thought to be helpful for children with AS. It wasn't until Brittney began to spend more time away from her parents that it seemed essential that she and others know the exact nature of her social, communication and behavioral difficulties. Now that her grandmother knows the nature of her difficulties she uses ignoring to overlook Brittney's occasional inappropriate comments rather than responding with a negative comment. She has also relinquished the teaching of self-care skills to Brittney's parents. She is now less anxious about her granddaughter's future, knowing that maturity is developmental and that while she has always been a little behind she still has plenty of time to become an adult.

The explanation

Living and working in a family requires open and honest communication; of course honesty does not always equate to diplomacy, which is often required when wanting social relationships to go well.

In Brittney's situation her parents learned over the years how to adapt family life to meet her needs and make family life bearable. Unfortunately, this was not as easily understood or transferred to the extended family, especially the grandmother. In Brittney's story her grandmother lacked a clear understanding of the nature of her social, communication, and behavioral difficulties. The lack of understanding caused her to apply what she knew about typical child development to this situation. It was this lack of understanding and misapplied strategies that led to poor social interactions between the grandmother and granddaughter. It was also stressful for the entire family.

It was the grandmother's impression that Brittney was either not taught, or refused to comply with what had been taught, regarding the correct way to care for her belongings. She thought that with additional guidance and, at times, ridicule that Brittney would just pick up on the cues and develop a desire and ability to care for her belongings. Unfortunately this type of teaching was not exactly what she needed. Brittney's grandmother needed a better understanding of the nature of her granddaughter's difficulties in order to address the immature behaviors in a more effective way.

The challenge for Brittney and her grandmother is all too familiar to families with teens and adults with AS. When a child is born with a disability it is typical for the parents and extended family to have doubts—doubts regarding the nature of the problem, the severity of the problem, the diagnosis given for the problem or even whether a problem exists at all. Every family member will have to arrive at some level of understanding and acceptance in accordance with their own capacity to deal with the unexpected. Understanding and acceptance is just the beginning of effective communication between family members. In addition to understanding and acceptance, family members will also need to learn how to communicate and interact with each other.

Communication is the basis for understanding between people. In order for communication between people to be effective, it must be understood by the speaker and listener. Communicating clearly and effectively is hard work. Family members frequently take each other for granted, thinking, at some level, that the other person will always be there and will always love me no matter what happens. This is probably true; you can love someone deeply and not always like them; but over time poor communication will wear on the quality of the relationship. A laissez faire attitude can lead to a lack of effort on the part of each family member to exert the energy necessary to communicate effectively and meaningfully.

The solution

The solution to quality relationships between family members is good communication. The steps to better communication are as follows:

1.   Establish an attitude of willingness to improve communication and social interaction between you and your family. This can be difficult because you may have hurt feelings or anger towards family members resulting from poor interactions in the past. Getting beyond past grievances is difficult, but it is possible.

2.   Carry out an honest appraisal of your contribution to past grievances or communication difficulties. The hardest part of this step is remaining focused on your own contribution to the social and communication difficulties. You need to remember that you can only change yourself; you cannot change another person. For this reason it is important to record your thoughts to provide a visual record for analysis using "An Honest Appraisal" in My Journal on page 180.

3.   Evaluate your social and communication skills using the appraisal. You may discover that you have failed in some way as the speaker or listener. You may discover that you have not extended the effort required to maintain good communication with family members or, if difficulties have arisen, you may discover that you neglected to apologize or seek some type of remedy for the miscommunication. If this is the case you may choose to ask the family member to forgive you and allow you to have a fresh start. It is true that communication difficulties are part of living with AS, so difficulties will occur. It is also true that people typically respond favorably to an apology, and are generally open to extending a fresh start to anyone who wants to try.

4.   Select strategies that will assist you in improving your communication in the areas that you have identified as problematic. As a speaker you will need to:

    ○ Use clear and concise language.

    ○ Be sensitive to include paralinguistic cues that increase your meaning.

○ Be sure to support your message with nonverbal cues.

○ Attend to the listener and modify your message if needed.

○ Be sensitive to the rules of conversation.

And as a listener you will need to:

○ Use effective listening (Chapter 6, Adaptive Tools).

○ Rephrase what you have heard.

○ Ask questions if unsure.

○ Be sensitive to the rules of conversation.

5. Be authentic with your family members. Share your struggles, hopes, and dreams. Tell them how they can help you and then be open to receiving the help. If you do not want help in a specific situation communicate that politely. You will want to use diplomacy rather than brutal honesty with family members just as you would with anyone with whom you hope to have a successful relationship. Diplomacy refers to a tactful and subtle way of interacting with people. In this way you can express yourself while considering the needs of others.

THE TOPIC: FRIENDS

Friends are two or more people involved in a relationship that includes mutual love, respect, trust, and unconditional acceptance for each other. The key term in the definition of the word "friend" is "mutual." The term "mutual" means that something is shared in common. In the definition of friend, it is love, respect, trust, and greater generosity that are shared in common. When people consider themselves to be friends, this usually implies that they have been able to identify interests that they have in common.

Friends are generally cooperative and supportive of each other. They spend time together engaged in their common interests. They are interested in each other's well-being and they ask questions of each other. After asking a question they wait and listen intently to the answer. They help each other even when it is inconvenient for them, or when they would just rather do something else. They try to understand when their friend makes a mistake or has an opinion that differs from their own. Friends are loyal to each other and they practice placing each other's interests over their own. Friends help each other, try to understand each other, are loyal to each other, and provide each other with company.

Friendships generally do not involve romantic interests, although friendships can progress to more intimate relationships involving romantic interest. If either person discovers that a friendship has progressed to a romantic interest, it is essential that both people share the same desire or the friendship will be jeopardized. There is nothing more complicated than one friend becoming romantically interested in another when the feelings are not reciprocated.

It is important to know that not every person will place the same level of importance on having friends. Some people are most comfortable with one friend while others may prefer a group of friends. Some teens and adults with AS may prefer not to have friends at all. In this case the family of the teen or adult may be more concerned about her having friends than she is herself.

It is important to know that the benefits of having friends, for those who want them, can be many. Friends can make life less boring. They can provide fun and excitement through companionship and recreation. They give advice and can be supportive during difficult times. It is believed that people who have friends are less lonely, happier, have a higher self-esteem and are more successful.

The challenge

> After work I was so tired that I decided to take the children out to a local restaurant for dinner rather than cooking. When we entered the restaurant we bumped into Miss Shelly, Ian's third grade teacher. We hadn't

seen Miss Shelly for several years. Ian was now 14 years of age and in the eighth grade. Miss Shelly was interested in Ian's transition from primary to middle school. She was asking lots of questions that lead me to think that she was most interested in his social adjustment to the new setting full of teenagers. While we talked, Ian listened, although he didn't act like he was listening. When given his opportunity to speak he began sharing about a new invention. He was spending a considerable amount of time thinking, planning and designing a safer tank for the army. In the middle of a sentence he changed topics and made the statement, "I don't know why nobody likes me." He rapidly returned to the topic of his invention. I attempted to respond to his statement that, to me, sounded like a question. I was wrong. Ian was not receptive to my probes. He shared his concern and desire for friends; however, it was his determination this was neither the place nor the time to go into any greater detail.

Jennifer, Ian's mom

P.S. Ian is a very smart and able student, especially in the area of mathematics. He is tall and handsome. By all outward appearances he should have no difficulty finding and maintaining friendships; however, he also has Asperger Syndrome. Ian's disability is displayed through his hyperactivity, strong and unusual pervasive interests, and what appears to others to be an intense self-absorption. These behaviors inhibit his ability to acquire and maintain friends.

The explanation

Ian's story is not unique; many teens and adults with AS would like to have a meaningful friendship, yet friendships are often elusive. It is a mistake to think every person with AS is nonsocial; the social behaviors just tend to look different. Social behaviors that look different may interfere with a person's ability to make friends. This interference can be viewed as something to overcome and does not have to be viewed as the final outcome. It is possible to progress in social awareness and competence, and this can lead to friendships for teens and adults with this desire.

There are teens and adults who are not concerned with having friends. This is a choice that teens and adults need to be able to make for themselves. Some people are happier without the social pressures and requirements of friendships. Recognizing these demands he or she may choose not to seek friendships and, in many cases, may choose not to seek romantic relationships. In this situation some people may prefer to strengthen family relationships or be satisfied with the acquaintances in their lives. If this is your preference do not be distressed; you will just want to focus on improving the quality of your relationships with family members and acquaintances if you have identified those as social areas of need.

For the parents or siblings of a teen or adult who does not want friendships, this can be difficult to understand. The family member will just have to work harder to take the perspective of their loved one on this topic and try to see the situation from his or her point of view. If family members do this, they will most likely begin to understand that the work involved in acquiring and maintaining friendships is just not how this person chooses to spend his energy.

In Ian's story he expresses a desire to have friends, but just isn't ready to deal with his issues related to friendships. There is a very good chance that he will become increasingly more interested and able as he gets older. His mother and other support people will need to watch, listen and be ready with opportunities to support his social progress when he indicates that he is ready. The truth is that most teens and adults with AS would enjoy having a friend and the benefits of a friendship, but lack the skills needed to establish and maintain friendships.

The solution

The steps to discovering friendships are as follows.

1. Study the requirements of a friendship. Friends are mutual relationships that require cooperation, loyalty, support of each other, sharing of common interests, spending time together, being interested in each other's well-being, helping each other, listening to each other, trying to understand each other, and placing the friend's interest ahead of your own.

2. Determine whether you would be a good friend.

   (a) Complete the "Would I make a good friend?" survey in My Journal on page 176.

   (b) If you answered "yes" to even a few of the statements on the friendship worksheet, you possess qualities important to being a good friend. Remember that you must be able to be a friend before you can have a friend and that friendships are more about the other person than they are about you. The good news is that, when you are a good friend, the feelings, thoughts, and behaviors extended are often returned many times over.

   (c) If you were unable to answer "yes" to any of the questions do not be discouraged. You may need to spend some time focusing on the skills required to be a friend. Or you may need to think more about your desire for a friend and the role that a friend would take in your life. Not everyone wants to have friends.

3. Compile a list of your personal interests by completing the "Personal Interest Survey" in My Journal on page 177. Remember that friendships are often based on mutual interests.

4. Now you are ready to look for a friend. You may find this person among people you already know, someone you go to school with, a person from work, someone you know

from a club or church, or someone living in your community. You will want to identify a person who has an interest or interests similar to yours. This will require you to observe, notice, and attend to other people in your social surroundings. In order to make friends you must pay attention to other people long enough to determine whether you have anything in common.

5.   When you identify a possible friend from your observations and it appears that you have a common interest, start a conversation on that topic. It would be best to prepare a list of questions ahead of time to guide your conversation. You may want to make a bulleted list or draft an entire script. A list will prompt your memory and help keep you on topic when talking to a prospective friend.

A script will allow you to rehearse your conversation before you talk with the prospective friend, increasing your comfort with the coming conversation. You may choose to write a script that focuses on your interests alone or you may choose to include some self-disclosure. Self-disclosure is telling the other person about your disability for the purpose of clarifying behaviors or mannerisms that may have already revealed your difficulties. In many instances other people have already identified that a social problem exists because of the ease with which people with typical social skills detect problems with pragmatics. People typically respond well when they understand the nature of the problem. See "Lists and Scripts" in My Journal: on page 178.

6.   For the first get-together, it would be a good to limit the amount of time to assure success. Initiating friendships require that you focus attention on the other person and this can be exhausting for an extended amount of time. Ensure you focus on the known requirements of friendship during the time together, and bear the following checklist in mind:

- ° Be sure to talk, if this is appropriate for the event. It would not be appropriate to talk during a movie or extensively while watching a televised program or while playing a video game.

- ° Be sure to allow the other person to talk and don't interrupt.

- ° Be sure to listen when the other person is talking and then respond appropriately.

- ° Be kind and think about the needs of the other person.

- ° Make sure that, at the end of the get-together, you thank the prospective friend for hanging out and say that you hope that you can do it again sometime.

7. After a short time passes, possibly a week, it is okay to contact your new prospective friend. Remember that you want to be viewed as a faithful friend, not a burdensome buddy. Tell her that you had a great time and hope that she did also. You might ask her opinion on the get-together. If she says that it did not go well or if she implies that she really does not want to do it again, it would be best to ask her how the get-together might have gone better. Tell her that you want to know her impressions of how things went, in the hopes that it will go better next time, or so that you can learn from the experience. In the event that she contacts you first, follow the same guidelines.

8. Take some time to think about and reflect on the comments made by your prospective friend. Think and reflect about your own observations. Write down any ideas that you think will improve the situation or other situations in the future. You might choose to share these ideas with the prospective friend or with others you know well.

9.   In the event that the first attempt is not successful be sure to continue the quest for a friend. Don't be discouraged if you have to repeat these steps many times before finding a friend. Many people go through their entire lives with only one or two friends, and they consider themselves blessed.

THE TOPIC: DATING

Dating is two people making plans to go out socially with one another, often out of romantic interest. In many cultures dating allows two people to spend time together for the purpose of determining if they might be suitable for marriage.

There are many different viewpoints on dating, ranging from casual dating, which allows the participants to date several people during the same time span, to exclusive dating which means that each participant will date only the other. The wide range of views on the topic of dating makes it a particularly difficult social relationship to navigate for everyone, but especially for teens and adults with AS.

While dating is not important to everyone, it is important to many teens and adults, including those with AS. Dating is frequently experienced during adolescence and adulthood, making it a social behavior that most people are interested in pursuing. People generally date because they have a desire for a social, emotional, and physical relationship with a person of the opposite sex. They may be interested in marriage and having children. Dating is essential to getting to know another person well enough to determine whether he or she is suitable for marriage. Dating can also provide companionship.

The challenge

High school was ending and it was time to graduate. Only two months to go and it would all be over. I had mixed feelings about graduating because these had been the best and the worst years of my life. The kids were mean and the teasing was relentless, the work was okay, but my friendship with Meredith was the best. Meredith and I had been friends since we were three years old. We grew up in houses right next to each other. Our parents were friends and played cards together a couple times a month. Meredith was always kind to me and made a point to talk to me every day even when the other kids were teasing or ignoring me. She was also incredibly hot. I knew that once school ended Meredith would be going away to college and that I would only see her during the summer. I really had a crush on her and wanted to ask her out on a date. I decided that I should ask her to go to the senior prom. I wasn't exactly sure what to say and I really struggled to handle the anxiety that I felt when she was around. I knew that she would say "no," but I had to take a chance. I knew that there was no way that I could do this without some help so I asked my mom to help me write out a script and I rehearsed what I wanted to say. I practiced the script over and over until I had it memorized. Time was running out so, on the last day that prom tickets were on sale, I decided to go for it and walked up to Meredith at her locker and began to recite my script. I started by saying, "I know that you are probably busy or you already have a date, but I uh uh uh." Meredith rescued my by finishing my sentence. She said, "But, I would like to ask you to go with me to the prom?" She then said "yes." I couldn't believe what I was hearing. I immediately turned around and walked away. It was a good thing that she knew me well enough to ring my house later that evening to ask for the specifics of the date, since those were the important details that I neglected to address when making the date. We ended up going to the dance together. It was our only "official" date. That night Meredith asked that we remain just friends. I like her enough to be okay with that arrangement.

Brett

P.S. Brett is a fairly insightful teenager who has the same desire as many other young men, to date the pretty girl next door. His anxiety about asking for a date is fairly typical for young men as they begin to develop the social communication skills required for dating. In Brett's situation he had the benefit of a long-standing friendship with a neighbor girl who recognized his difficulties and responded in a kind manner. He also prepared ahead of time by writing and rehearsing a conversation script. This helped him, but what helped him even more was the fact that Meredith knew him well enough to assist him in making this difficult first step. In Brett's situation the specific senior dance dilemma was solved, but Brett's dating difficulties remain.

The explanation

Interest in dating is fairly common for teens and adults with AS, although the onset of this interest frequently occurs later than with neurotypical teens. This lag in socialization is sometimes called "extended adolescence." An interest in dating may not develop until adulthood.

The thought of dating can be painful for the person with AS who wants to date, but is hindered by awkward social skills that often overshadow desirable traits that would be attractive to others. Another hindrance to dating is the inability to identify and accurately interpret nonverbal signals. Someone who is interested in you will often attempt to gain your attention through nonverbal cues like smiles, eye contact, and flirtatious posture to see if his or her interest is returned. This pretest minimizes the degree of risk of rejection when asking the person for a date. The flirtation before the actual date is much like a dance that relies almost entirely on nonverbal communication. For someone who has significant difficulty interpreting nonverbal communication these signals go undetected and unreturned. This is cause enough for the person to discontinue the pursuit.

Women with AS are more likely to date than men for two reasons. In most cultures men are expected to initiate dating and this requires a high degree of self-confidence along with a willingness to risk rejection. The difference in social requirements makes it far more difficult for a man to date than a woman.

The more successful dating relationships generally occur between two people with AS rather than between a person with AS and one that is neurotypical. There are fewer women diagnosed with AS than men so a woman with AS has a greater chance of meeting a compatible man with AS than a man has of meeting a compatible woman.

The solution

Study the topic and develop an understanding of the purpose and requirements, along with specific skills required in the dating process. Dating is two people making plans to go out socially with one another, often out of romantic interest. In many cultures dating is for the purpose of determining whether the other person is suitable for marriage. Opinions on dating range significantly between people, depending upon their culture and other life experiences. It is common that people differ in their viewpoints on dating. Some may view initial dating in the same category as hanging out with a sibling, while others may view it as a precursor to marriage. The wide range of perspectives and opinions makes dating a very complicated social relationship. The most important thing to remember when developing an understanding of dating is that there are no hard and fast rules. The key to successful dating for the person with AS is to communicate clearly and with diplomacy the perimeters for the dating relationship.

Specific skills required for successful dating generally include the ability to identify flirtatious nonverbal signals or have a good friend who will serve as your nonverbal flirtation observer and who will tell you when someone is flirting with you; the ability to share your time and resources; the capacity to care for the well-being of the other person; an ability and desire to share interests; the ability to communicate using diplomacy; and the ability to see another person's point of view or the ability to ask questions and seek solutions to problems that arise when you struggle to see the other person's perspective. To prepare yourself for dating, take the following steps.

1.   Explore your interests in dating by completing the "What about Dating?" survey in My Journal on page 181. This survey will help you identify your contribution to a dating relationship, the issues of marriage and the perimeters for a dating relationship based on your values and tolerances.

2.   Identify and list places to meet a suitable partner. Most books written on successful marriages state that common interests are essential to good relationships. Based on this information good locations for finding potential partners would include work, school, church, community groups, hobbyist organizations, sporting clubs, and through friends. In all of these settings you are likely to find people with interests similar to yours.

3.   Meeting someone with shared interests and attitudes on dating is critical. You will want to be sure that, as the dating progresses, you use your diplomatic conversational skills to talk about key issues. For example, if you have decided that you are not ready for an exclusive relationship, then it is important to share that information with the person you are dating, not immediately but some time early in the relationship. This can be difficult, but more problems arise from the lack of communication than from clear, diplomatic communication. If you rely on a friend to introduce you to someone to date or assist you in identifying nonverbal signals, be sure that it is someone you can trust and who has a good reputation.

4. Dating is a time to talk and share experiences, dreams, hopes, and desires. It is a time for the couple to explore their compatibility with the prospect of a potential marriage. It is important to know that people generally present their best behavior while courting. For example, your date may laugh at all of your jokes, she may not want to be seen without her make-up, or you avoid taking her to your apartment because you really do not want her to see that you are messy. For these reasons it can be challenging to sort through the outward behavior to see the real person, although it is essential that you see and accept each other as you are before committing to a long-term relationship.

THE TOPIC: MARRIAGE

Marriage is an interpersonal relationship that is generally intimate and sexual. It is recognized by religious, social, and governmental entities. The most common form of marriage unites a man and a woman as husband and wife. People marry for many reasons, but usually for one or more of the following: legal, social, and economic reasons; the formation of a family unit; procreation and the education and nurturing of children; legitimizing sexual relations; and/or public declaration of love.

Many adults with AS marry and when they do they find the same challenges in marriage as those without AS. They discover that in order to maintain a good marriage there must be hard work, communication and the ability to understand the thoughts and feelings of the other person. Clear communication assists the person as he or she attempts to identify the needs of the other person. This provides each person with what he or she needs to be successful in the marriage without having to become a "mind reader."

In a marriage it is important to communicate your needs, desires, and intentions rather than waiting and hoping that your partner will develop the mental telepathy to know what you need and want without you telling him or her. This minimizes the number of times that you will be disappointed because your spouse cannot consistently or accurately interpret your needs. This is problematic when it occurs in any marriage, but it is especially difficult if you are a person with AS. You may not perceive the undeclared need of your spouse or the angry nonverbal communication which can cause your spouse to become extremely confused and frustrated.

The National Healthy Marriage Center (2008) summarizes what marriage scholars have emphasized as the ten key elements of a healthy marriage:

1. *Commitment*: Spouses have a long-term perspective. They intend to persevere when troubles come up, and they are willing to sacrifice some of their personal needs for each other.

2. *Satisfaction*: Overall, individuals are happy and satisfied with their relationship. This does not mean that the marriage has no problems and challenges.

3. *Communication*: Couples interact with each other to exchange information and solve problems in respectful, positive ways.

4. *Effective conflict resolution*: Almost all couples have serious disagreements. How they handle these disagreements can make the difference between a healthy and unhealthy relationship.

5. *Lack of violence and abuse*: Even though conflict is a normal part of marriage, aggression and violence indicate an unhealthy relationship.

6. *Sexual fidelity or faithfulness*: Spouses do not have intimate physical relationships outside the bonds of marriage.

7. *Friendship and spending time together*: In a healthy marriage, couples enjoy being together. They are friends. They respect each other and enjoy each other's company.

8. *Intimacy and emotional support:* Couples in a healthy marriage are physically and emotionally intimate with each other. They trust, care for, and love each other.

9. *Commitment to children:* In a healthy marriage with children, the couple is committed to the development and well-being of all their children.

10. *Duration/Permanence:* Believing that marriage is permanent and that the relationship will last helps to sustain a healthy marriage.

(NHMRC 2008)

The challenge

I was not diagnosed with AS until I was 45 years old after my wife Theresa and I started marriage counseling. She insisted that we get help to learn to communicate with each other and she finally decided that she was going to divorce me if I would not go to talk to a marriage counselor. I really didn't want the marriage to end because I didn't want to be alone again, but I just wasn't sure that a counselor could help.

I didn't get married until I was 42 because I was very involved in my career and, to tell you the truth, not many women were interested in dating me. I met Theresa at work and, if I were truthful, she was my first real girlfriend. She asked me out on our first date. If she had waited for me to ask her out on a date we would have never gotten together. I had given up on dating many years earlier because it just wasn't worth the threat of rejection. I think that if she had waited for me it would have never happened. I didn't even know that she was interested in me until she asked me out for coffee after a concert. After the first date we saw each other every day. We decided that it made sense to get married so we could share expenses and be a family. It didn't take much to convince me because I was tired of living alone.

Being married hasn't been easy. Theresa seems to be mad at me all the time and I never know why so I just ignore her most of the time. When I ask her what is bothering her she says that I get lost in my work and that living with me makes her feel lonely. When I do suggest that we do something together she says that I am bossy. I just can't seem to get it right. I am either ignoring her or too bossy. I am also very forgetful and disorganized. She has a strong need to have an orderly home so she gets very angry with me when I leave my clothes and other things around the apartment. I really want this marriage to work, but I just do not know how to make her happy.

Samuel

P.S. Samuel is an accomplished musician and composer. He is paid well for his musical talents. He met his wife while working. She too is an accomplished musician. Theresa was mesmerized by Samuel's many talents. She thought that his tendencies to be aloof and eccentric were endearing qualities found only in people with great genius. After a short courtship the married couple settled into daily life. Theresa soon discovered that Samuel's aloofness and his eccentric qualities challenged communication. Samuel tried to address Theresa's complaint that she was lonely, but wasn't able to find the right balance between alone time and couples time without sounding bossy. He agreed to marriage counseling. After several visits to the counselor Samuel agreed to seek an evaluation with an adult psychiatrist who diagnosed him with AS. Now the couple is trying to understand how Sam's disability impacts the relationship and what they can do to make things better.

The explanation

Many adults with AS marry and when they do they find the same challenges in marriage as those without AS. The challenges include hard work, communication, and understanding the thoughts and feelings of your spouse (called mind reading). Unfortunately, two of the three challenges listed are particularly difficult for individuals with AS, these are communication and understanding the thoughts and feelings of the other person.

The problems that Samuel and Theresa are experiencing in their marriage are related to communication and mind reading. Prior to his diagnosis Theresa insisted that Samuel identify and interpret her thoughts and feelings without the benefit of conversation. He was then expected to respond to her needs in a manner that she thought was appropriate. His inability to read her mind caused her to view him as distant and insensitive. Prior to the marriage she viewed these same traits as endearing and creative. It is common in marriage for a person to change his or her views of certain behaviors when during the courtship the same behaviors were embraced or overlooked. The same behaviors that Theresa found endearing are now the behaviors that she wants to change. Changing expectations once married can be confusing for the spouse with AS. In fairness to Theresa neither she nor Samuel were prepared for the challenges of married life.

In this scenario Samuel recognizes and acknowledges that problems exist and that he is contributing to the discord. He is also learning that his struggles are not character defects, but result from a neurodevelopmental disability. The couple is learning that changes are possible with the help from others.

It is important for individuals with AS to recognize that romantic and intimate relationships will require hard work. The divorce rate for men and women with AS is very high, some say as high as 80 percent of all marriages end in divorce. The percentages are lower for couples who both have AS or other social disabilities. In either case a successful long-term marriage is rare and for this reason it is critical that the couple affected by AS embrace the idea of hard work and solicit support from others who can encourage, support, and guide the couple towards marital maturity.

The solution

To improve or maintain the quality of a marriage for individuals with AS each person must commit him or herself to work hard.

- Pre-marital counseling helps couples learn more about each other and develop the skills necessary for communicating in a marriage. It is important that counseling sessions take place over a period of months and be used to discuss more than the marriage ceremony. Pre-marital counseling services can be provided through agencies, private providers, and ministers.

- Establishing a schedule for assessing each person's level of satisfaction in the marriage could be a useful strategy for recognizing and acknowledging problems early. Early detection of problems can provide the couple with time to seek support and employ remedies before loosing hope. This could take place weekly or monthly. It would involve taking an inventory of your own contribution to the marriage over the past week or month followed by a discussion on how you might do better. This approach is preferred to the typical way that couples discuss their grievances which generally involves taking the inventory of the other person and then telling them how they can improve. It is more advantageous and less frustrating to focus your energy on changing yourself rather than trying to change your spouse.

- Marriage education can offer training in specific skills required in a marriage. These include learning to talk without fighting, skills in problem solving, exercises to strengthen trust and commitment, household management skills, financial management and decision making, and learning how to take better care of each other.

- Marriage counseling or therapy can offer advice and encouragement, wisdom and insight into each other and the marriage, learning to goal set, development of skills in conflict resolution, and issues related to intimacy. We often think that we can solve our own problems, but this may not always be true. Marital difficulties are more likely to resolve if the counseling occurs before becoming chronic. Be sure to identify a marriage counselor with a strong understanding of autism spectrum disorders.

THE TOPIC: PARENTING

Parenting is the process of raising and educating a child from birth until adulthood. Most western countries identify the legal end of a parent's commitment to their child at age 18 years, but that does not diminish the feeling of commitment and responsibility that extends beyond this point for many parents.

It is the responsibility of parents to provide for the physical, emotional, and intellectual needs of the child they are raising, by providing protection, shelter, clothing, healthy nourishment, healthcare, education, training, love, and a sense of belonging. Parenting is a job that lasts 24 hours a day, 7 days a week for a minimum of 18 years. "Becoming a parent is the most challenging job you'll ever have, but it's also the most incredible adventure life has to offer (Becoming Parents Program 2006).

The challenge

I am a mother with AS. My husband and I have two children aged five and seven years. People often ask me what it is like to be a mother with AS and I am never really sure how to respond because my only experience is being a mom with AS. I do not know how my experience differs from other mothers. I would say that being a mother has been challenging, but I suppose that is true for every mother. When I discovered that I was pregnant I decided that I needed to learn everything that I could about children and parenting. I was concerned that I wouldn't just pick it up, so I made it a course of study. I attended parenting classes and I subscribed to three different parenting magazines. I read the magazines from cover to cover and then cut out articles that I thought were important.

My husband is very good at helping me with the boys, but I am generally responsible for getting them to school, to activities and their appointments. Keeping organized is my biggest problem. I have devised a sticky note system for keeping track of appointments. I have a calendar on the refrigerator. I write everything down on sticky notes and stick them on the refrigerator. Everyone in the household knows that they can look on the refrigerator to find out anything about our schedule. A concern from other people was whether I would be able to socialize my children and I am fairly sure that I am doing an okay job. My children attend school and participate in a few other activities. Sometimes they have friends over, but generally we are a family that keeps to ourselves. Everyone seems pretty happy with this arrangement. In the event that I hear concerns from school or from others regarding the boys' socialization I will do whatever needs to be done to assure that this is addressed. I don't have to be the one who socializes them as long as I can provide the opportunities and experiences that they require.

Sondra

P.S. Sondra is the mother of two and she has AS. Her husband is helpful and supportive with the children. When becoming pregnant she became concerned that she might not know how to parent her children. She decided that the best way to address this was to study everything that she could about children and parenting. She has devised an organizational system that works for her family and one that she can teach her boys to use as they get older.

The explanation

Parenting is a full-time job. Caring for the needs of a child from birth to adulthood takes an enormous amount of time, energy, and resources. Sondra is concerned that she might not have the knowledge or background to be an effective parent. She recognizes the enormity of the task and accurately predicts her potential to struggle with this important task.

To compensate for her lack of intuitive understanding of parenting Sondra devises a plan to strengthen her knowledge and preparation for becoming a parent. She reads and gathers important resources and designs a simple system to keep organized. Her approach to this new challenge is to use her good cognitive skills to compensate for her less perceptive social and relational skills. She is aware of her children's needs for social and relational opportunities, so she provides them as she is able and she monitors the situation knowing that she may need to rely on assistance from others if her boys demonstrate a need in this area.

Another area of concern for individuals with AS who become parents is financial. Many adults with AS are unemployed or underemployed. This significantly minimizes the resources that parents need to raise children. When this occurs parents may find themselves relying on external family or government support. This can be stressful to parents who want to offer their children the resources they need to flourish.

The solution

Parenting is challenging for everyone, but this is especially true for the parent with AS. Specific areas of difficulty may include emotionally relating to your children, providing needed structure and physical care, modeling and teaching appropriate social behaviors, providing socializing opportunities, and providing the resources that children need to flourish.

- A cognitive approach to parenting is a good place to start. The cognitive model refers to the development of mental representations of parenting that can be developed from acquired knowledge. A mental representation refers to the way things typically occur. For example children get hungry and need a wholesome well-balanced diet to grow and be healthy. This generally requires three prepared meals each day with small snacks at other times. For a parent who may only eat twice a day, this departure from routine may require significant planning. This approach is highly systematic and works to gather information related to the needs of the child and the roles and responsibilities of the parents to meet the child's needs. This knowledge can be acquired through child development and child care classes in the community or on-line, by talking to family members, friends and acquaintances about child rearing practices, by observing and reflecting on the parenting practices of others, and reading and studying books and articles on the topic.

- Be open to comments and ideas from others recognizing that you may have blinders in certain areas of parenting.

- Be willing to locate and provide your children with opportunities and experiences that they will require to develop well in all areas, especially those areas in which you may lack skills or confidence.

- Be observant of your children. Ask them when you are unsure of their needs or well-being. If your child is young she may not be able to express her needs so you will be required to interpret her behavior as her form of communication. All behavior is communication and for the preverbal or young child this may provide you with the only insight into her needs. If you struggle to accurately interpret the behavior ask a friend, family member or the child's teacher to assist you in interpreting the behavior. Keep a journal of her behaviors to keep track of her communication style. By recording behaviors you will begin to identify patterns of communication that will make it easier to interpret future behaviors. Use "Behavior as Communication" in My Journal to record your observations on page 183.

- Communicate with your spouse about your concerns and efforts to be a good parent. Ask them to join you in this endeavor. If they are not completely on-board with your plan ease them into the plan over time by providing helpful and useful information when needed.

- Seek support from others including your family, church, and community organizations.

THE TOPIC: STRANGERS

Strangers are people with whom one has not had any social contact. They are usually people who are not members of family, although unfamiliar family members could be strangers. While we often think of strangers as dangerous because of the "stranger warnings" taught by parents to their children, in reality all people we do not know or have not met yet are strangers. So the difficulty is to determine which people who would be classified as strangers are people that we will soon know as acquaintances or friends, and which people we should avoid. It is probably best to err on the side of caution. If you do not know someone, assume that he or she cannot be trusted, until you verify his or her trustworthiness. Do not give out your personal or financial information or go anywhere with people in the category of "stranger."

The challenge

I work as a hostess in a fast food restaurant. It is my job to keep the tables clean, the trash off the floor and the condiment bar straightened. I like organizing the condiment bar best and people often compliment me on my orderliness. I like working at the restaurant because I feel good about my job. The people I work with are my friends. One late night when I was working, a man kept trying to talk to me and was saying that I was a pretty girl. My boss told him to leave me alone because I was working. He left the restaurant that night, but starting coming into the restaurant every day. Every time he would come in he would say hello to me. He usually did not eat dinner, but always drank a cup of coffee. A couple of weeks went by and he asked me to go out for a drink at the bar next to the restaurant. I wanted to go and made plans to meet him outside of the restaurant after work.

My boss overheard our conversation and told me that he did not think that it was a good idea for me to go out with this man before I got to know him because he was a stranger. I didn't think that he was a stranger because he was very nice and I saw him every day. My boss told me that I needed to do something to "check-out" this guy. I wasn't really sure what he meant by "check-out" this guy so I asked my sister what this meant. She got very upset at me for talking to a strange man at work. She told me that the man was a stranger because I did not know him and she said that his comments were suspicious because it was not polite to say that I was a pretty girl and to bother me at work.

This man is a stranger because I didn't know anything about him and my sister said that he was suspicious. This scared me so I decided that I didn't want to go on a date with him. I didn't want to see him anymore, but I knew he would come back to my work. When I saw him I told him I couldn't go out with him, but he kept trying to get me to go by saying please, you are so beautiful, and we will have such a good time. I was starting to feel afraid. I realized that I was having a problem so I looked back at my boss who came out of the kitchen and told the man to leave because I did not want to go on a date with him. The man said a few curse words and went away. I didn't ever see him again. I am glad that I had my boss and my sister to help me with this problem.

Candice

P.S. Candice is an attractive 24-year-old female who is hard working and well suited to her current job, although she is underpaid. Her job brings her into contact with the general public. She is kind, yet naive about her surroundings. She is flattered by the advances of a stranger and after a few short weeks is coerced into having a date with a stranger. Those around her are concerned because they noticed subtle traits and behaviors in the stranger that Candice is unaware of. She allows her boss to assist her in checking out the stranger to discover that he is not suitable to date.

The explanation

Identifying strangers, interpreting nonverbal communication and judging verbal communication may be a significant struggle for the teen or adult with AS, placing him or her in a vulnerable position and at considerable risk in identifying impending danger.

Identifying a person as a stranger can be problematic for the teen or adult with AS. To classify someone as a stranger, you must recognize that you have not met them before. This can be complicated since many individuals with AS struggle with facial recognition. Facial recognition involves looking at another person's face and eyes long enough to make a memory. Many people with AS find direct eye contact difficult so they avoid eye contact with others. It is the averting of eye contact that reduces the time committed to facial study, and therefore interferes with locking into memory the individual facial characteristics of the person. This reduces the likelihood that the person with AS will be able to distinguish between an acquaintance and a stranger. As for Candice she initially classified her suitor as a stranger based upon facial recognition. She recognized that she did not know this man; however, after seeing him a few times at work she modified her classification based upon the frequency of contact rather than an increase in information about the person.

A suspicious or even dangerous stranger may reveal his or her intentions through nonverbal communication such as body posture, movement and facial expression. Nonverbal cues can alert or signal an observer of the intentions of the stranger. Remember that people communicate through nonverbal communication even when they might not want to communicate. The human body when awake will communicate even without permission. The subtle nonverbal messages sent by a stranger would be difficult for many teens and adults with AS to interpret. Candice was unable to distinguish the stranger's nonverbal cues as dangerous, while her boss was able to identify subtle characteristics that alerted him to danger. Thankfully he shared his concerns with her and she agreed to seek more information about the stranger before the date. This may have prevented a horrible situation.

Judging the authenticity of verbal communication requires social reasoning and astuteness. This means that you will need to be able to hear the words a stranger says and interpret the truthfulness of the statement. In the scenario Candice struggles most to accurately assess the content of the stranger's flattery. He says, "You are such a pretty girl," and "You are so beautiful, and we will have such a good time." While she is not overly flattered by his comments she struggles to see the inappropriateness of his interrupting her at work, making sexual advances, and not taking "no" for an answer. For Candice her positive attributes of honesty and sense of fairness inhibit her ability to see the dishonesty in this other person. She is seen by the stranger as naive and gullible which places her at tremendous risk for abuse. Many criminals search for individuals who are unaware of their surroundings and unable to rapidly interpret danger.

Teenagers and adults with AS may become victim to strangers in several ways that include identity theft, property theft, robbery, extortion, swindling and assault.

The solution

Here are some steps you can take to stay safe with strangers:

1. Establish a list of personal rules for safety and hold tight to these rules regarding strangers. Prepare your personal set of rules by completing the "Personal Rules for Safety" in My Journal on page 182. An example of a personal list of rules might include the following:

   ° Do not talk to strangers.

   ° Do not accept gifts, money, or food from strangers.

   ° Do not take rides from strangers.

   ° Do not give personal or financial information to strangers.

   ° Do not let strangers touch your food or drink.

   ° Do not help strangers.

2. Establish a network of people who you know and trust for feedback on strangers. You might refer to these people as your "trusted allies." This might include your parents, siblings, teachers, colleagues, or employer. In the event that a stranger approaches you even after you have ignored them be sure to tell someone. Ask for an opinion on the stranger's motives. Factor the opinion into your

understanding of the stranger and be sure to adhere to your personal safety rules.

3.   Recognize that communicating on the internet allows people to say anything that they want to say, whether it is true or not. A person may say that they are young when they are old, that they are female when they are male, or that they are honest and caring when they might be a thief. It is hard to know when the person you talk to on the internet is who and what they say they are, so it is better to keep conversations with people on the internet impersonal.

   ◦   In the event that you talk to someone on-line who you think that you must meet; be sure that you have your trusted allies help you screen this person *before* providing them with any information that could be used to identify your location.

   ◦   Remember to let your allies know who you are talking to on-line. Never meet anyone alone that you have met on the internet until you have a chance to check-out their stories with reliable sources.

   ◦   Save copies of your conversations in case you want an ally to view the conversation.

4.   Practice your observation skills. While watching a movie or television program with a friend or family member select an actor to observe for a 10 or 15-minute time span. Conduct separate observations and compare them at the end of the selected time span. Use "Guide for Observing Body Language" in My Journal on page 185 to guide you in this activity. Observe the behavior and body language of the antagonist, opponent, or villain in the story. Note down your observations. Observe the behavior and body language of the protagonist, the main character who represents goodwill in the story. Note down your observations. Compare your observations looking most

carefully at the messages sent by the body language removed from the words.

It is fun to see if you can identify body language that is inconsistent with the spoken message, we usually classify this as bad acting. The nonverbal cues should match the spoken message unless it is the actor's intention to send mixed messages. Reflect upon the accuracy of your interpretation and continue to practice.

3   Health and Medical

Maintaining good physical and mental health is essential for overall social adjustment and well-being. People who are healthy and feel well have increased energy. If every person has a single beaker full of energy on any given day and that energy is depleted by poor nutrition, lack of exercise, poor sleep habits, and poor healthcare, that leaves far less energy to tackle the challenges that come from living and coping with AS.

In this chapter topics for healthy living are explored. The specific topics covered include nutrition, fitness and sleep, mental healthcare, and healthcare. Each topic is defined and the purposes of each topic are presented. Personal stories are told that describe the struggle and unique challenges that teens and adults with Asperger Syndrome experience related to healthy living. Practical solutions are presented in an easy-to-follow, step-by-step format to address each challenge.

THE TOPIC: NUTRITION, FITNESS AND SLEEP

Well-balanced nutrition, regular fitness and sleep are essential for good health. Adopting a balanced diet is essential to a person's health and well-being. No single food contains all the nutrients the body needs to be healthy and function efficiently. For this reason it is important to select a diet that contains a variety of foods that are eaten over a period of time to ensure sufficient intake of the nutrients needed for the body to function at the maximum level possible.

In order to have the energy we need to live our diet must include a balance between carbohydrates, fat, and protein. Too little protein can interfere with growth of hair and other body functions while too much protein can cause other organs, including the kidneys and liver, to be stressed. Too little fat can lead to obesity and infertility while too much fat can lead to obesity and heart disease. Too many carbohydrates can lead to obesity, breast cancer, diabetes, and heart attacks while too few carbohydrates can lead to fatigue, muscle cramps, and poor mental functioning. Inadequate intake of vitamins, minerals, and dietary fiber can lead to overall deficiencies and digestive problems.

The U.S. Department of Health and Human Services recommends in the *Dietary Guidelines for Americans* (2005) that people eat a variety of fruits and vegetables, whole-grain products, fat-free or low-fat milk products while reducing portion size, fat, processed sugar, and salt intake. It is important to include foods in your diet that provide you the essential vitamins, minerals, and dietary fiber. It is also important to drink water.

Regular physical exercise should be included in everyone's daily routine and is particularly important for young people. Exercise helps to build up stamina and strength and manage body weight. Swimming, cycling, skiing, jogging, aerobic dancing, and walking are all ways of staying fit, and some people enjoy the added social benefits of team sports. The American Heart Association and the American College of Sports Medicine (2007) guidelines on physical activity say that "all healthy adults ages 18–65 should be getting at least 30 minutes of moderate-intensity activity five days of the week."

Regular and rigorous exercise can lead to more restful sleep, reduce symptoms of anxiety and depression, and help people quit smoking and stay smoke-free, increase mental efficiency, and increase levels of sexual satisfaction. It can also help lower cholesterol and blood pressure and can reduce your risks for osteoporosis, diabetes, and heart disease.

Sleep is essential to your physical and emotional health. Studies have shown that without enough sleep, a person's ability to perform even simple tasks declines dramatically. A sleep-deprived individual may experience impaired performance, irritability, lack of concentration and daytime drowsiness (Killgore, Balkin and Wesenten 2006). The most common consequence of sleep loss is falling asleep while driving. One third of all drivers have fallen asleep at the wheel. The monetary cost is approximately 30 billion dollars annually and the human cost is roughly 100,000 crashes, 71,000 injuries, and 1500 fatalities a year (Wanf and Knipling 1994).

The typical number of hours of sleep required by teenagers and adults differs. The typical teenager requires 9.5 hours of sleep each night while the average adult requires 6 to 8 hours. The actual requirement for sleep varies from person to person. The increased need for sleep during the teenage years is generally attributed to the rapid growth and physical changes that occur during this stage. The amount of required sleep decreases as the body reaches maturity.

The signs of sleep deprivation include difficulty waking in the morning, falling asleep during the day, irritability in the afternoon, oversleeping on the weekend, having difficulty remembering or concentrating, waking up often and having trouble going back to sleep, moodiness, depression, and poor performance at school and work.

The benefits of sleep include faster and more complete recovery from illness or injury, reduced effects of stress, increased ability to concentrate, enhanced ability to handle minor irritations, improved memory, enhanced ability to perform tasks requiring logical reasoning and mathematical calculations, improved personal relationships, and increased hand-eye coordination.

The challenge

I have had sleep problems for as long as I can remember. I have never been able to fall asleep before 2:00 a.m. Even when I try to go to bed earlier I cannot fall asleep. My mind just races from one thing to another. This is a huge problem for me now because I am in college and sometimes I have 8:00 a.m. classes. I am usually able to wake up for class, but I am tired all day. I have trouble staying organized and I am not taking very good care of myself. I know that I need more sleep, but can't seem to figure out how to get tired sooner.

Sam

The explanation

Issues of nutrition, fitness, and sleep are frequently a concern to those who care for the well-being of a teen or adult with AS, but often less of a concern for those with AS. The lesser concern is not always because the individuals do not recognize the benefits of healthy living, but because he or she is adapted or responding in the best way they know how.

Olfactory and tactile sensitivities along with a desire for sameness frequently minimize tolerance for varied food choices. A narrow range and limited number of food choices can cause nutritional concerns. Diets high in refined processed sugars, like cakes, donuts, or cookies, or those high in fat like cheese pizza and chicken nuggets can lead to lethargy that inhibits the desire to engage in exercise or other fitness activities. Motor difficulties often inhibit the desire to participate in team sports and frequently inhibit the desire to exercise in general.

Sleep deprivation is a common experience for many teens and adults with AS. A large percentage of individuals with AS have difficulty with getting to sleep at night, waking in the morning and feeling sleepy during the day (Bruni 2007). The reason for these sleep difficulties has not been determined, but some suspect that the cause is related to the neurological nature of AS and its impact on sleep cycles (Bruni 2007).

Nutrition, fitness, and sleep are interrelated. Good nutrition is required for fitness and fitness improves sleep. All three improve health and influence your overall sense of well-being.

The solution

Steps to healthy living

Gather the facts on your current habits and patterns related to nutrition, fitness, and sleep. This will require observation and careful noting. Chart your habits for one week. Write down everything you eat and drink, the total number of minutes given to fitness activities including walking, housework, and exercise. Calculate the total number of hours of sleep per night and divide the hours of sleep by the number of nights to determine the average number of hours of sleep per week. Use "Steps in Healthy Living" in My Journal on page 188 to chart your behaviors.

Many people with AS have other medical problems. For this reason it is essential that you seek advice from your physician or medical advisor before acting on any of the suggestions in this section and in this book. After charting your behaviors, look at each category separately.

Nutrition

Given what you now know about healthy nutrition, rate your current eating habits—one for excellent, two for fair, and three for poor. If you selected the rating of either two or three you may want to consider a change.

Start by selecting one item from the processed, refined sugar list or fat list to reduce and one item from the grains, fruits, vegetables, or dairy to add or increase. Continue adding healthy foods and deleting unhealthy foods until you believe that you have achieved a balanced diet.

Fitness

Given what you now know about fitness rate your current exercise habits—one for excellent, two for fair and three for poor. If you selected the rating of either two or three you may want to consider a change.

Start by increasing your activity and movement by 30 minutes one day each week. Continue to add some type of movement until you are engaging in some type of fitness activity for 30 minutes, five days each week. You could:

- Walk or bike to school or work.

- Add housework to your duties.

- Work on the garden or lawn.

- Take the stairs instead of the elevator.

- Schedule exercise time.

- Join a fitness center and go.

- Walk during your lunch break at school or work.

- Get off the bus or subway one stop from home and walk the rest of the way.

- Ask someone to take a walk with you.

- Exercise to a DVD or computer program.

- Walk the dog.

- Go swimming

Sleep

Given what you now know about sleep requirements rate your current sleep habits—one for excellent, two for fair, and three for poor. If you selected the rating of either two or three you may want to consider a change.

Start by writing a sleep hygiene plan. A sleep hygiene plan is a carefully designed routine that supports sleep.

1. Decide the ideal amount of sleep you need to function at your best.

2. Determine the time that you must wake up each day and count backwards the number of hours you need to sleep.

3. Set that time as your official "bedtime."

4. Establish rules for yourself around sleep, bedtime, and the bedroom. To create a soothing bedtime routine to start in advance of your official "lights out" bedtime, you could: read a good book; use a heating pad; dress in comfy clothes, and turn off all technology.

    Bed is for sleeping, not eating, smoking, your computer, listening to music, or watching television. It's best not to exercise or shower right before bedtime unless you know that this makes you sleepy, and also refrain from drinking caffeinated drinks and minimize alcohol. Be in bed with "lights out" at the designated bedtime to create a good bedtime routine.

5. If your mind races, meditate, pray, or try repeating in your mind a soothing poem. Sometimes gently rocking back and forth can be soothing.

6. Stay in bed until morning. If you must get up for the restroom try to do so with minimal interruption; maybe you could place a nightlight in the bathroom so that you do not need to turn on a bright bulb.

7. Be active during the day and eat healthily. This promotes good sleep.

THE TOPIC: MENTAL HEALTHCARE

Mental health is a state of well-being in which we realize our own potential, can cope with the normal stresses of life, can work productively and fruitfully, and are able to make a contribution to our community. Our well-being consists of our happiness, confidence, and general outlook on life.

Identifying your potential comes directly from an accurate assessment of your skills, talents, strengths, and limitations. This is not something that you already are, but what you can realistically become given your current capabilities. The ability to cope with the normal stresses of life refers to the capacity to endure challenges and alleviate problems when possible. Working productively and fruitfully refers to the ability to identify the type of work for which you are best suited, develop the capabilities required for the work, and locate a setting where productivity is possible. Contributing to your community refers to giving something of yourself to others. It involves your role in the betterment of your community. Your giving can come through physical and tangible gifts or a general sense that the world is a better place because you lived well.

Good mental health can be difficult to achieve and even harder to maintain. Threats to mental health include stress, mental illness, and disability. Stress can be physical stress resulting from illness or injury and/or emotional stress resulting from loss, concerns with safety, worries about finances, school demands, employment challenges, social problems, and loneliness. Chronic stress can lead to health problems and can alienate you from others.

Mental illness is a disturbance of the mind that may interfere with normal behavior and make daily life difficult. There are many different types of mental illness, with anxiety and depression the most common. Anxiety is the feeling of excessive worry and tension along with the anticipation of pending doom. Anxiety is marked by physiological symptoms such as heart palpitations, sweating, trembling, fatigue, headaches, muscle tension, nausea, and difficulty swallowing.

Depression is persistent feelings of sadness, pessimism, worthlessness, and hopelessness that last for more than a few days. It is also the loss of interest in favored activities and the loss of caring about yourself and others. Experiencing feelings of sadness for a short period of time or in a low degree is pretty normal. Feeling sad for a period of weeks at a level that interferes with life functioning could be indicative of clinical depression.

The challenges that come from living with a disability can also threaten good mental health. For the teen or adult with AS social and communication problems can lead to chronic frustration, isolation, dependence, unemployment, and underemployment that undermine overall wellness, including mental health.

The challenge

> I am 28 years old and I see no hope for my future. I have tried my best to do everything that I can to get ahead. I was a pretty good student in high school and I was able to graduate from college. I work from home as a free-lance writer and this is good because I just don't have the energy to deal with people anymore. I have always strug-gled to cope with other people, but it is particularly diffi-cult for me now. I have a few magazine contracts, but I am finding it hard to muster the energy to meet my dead-lines. I am at risk of losing at least one of the contracts. I have always had a tendency to be a little depressed, but I think that this is the worst. I really can't identify any partic-ular thing that is making me feel sad, I just feel sad.
>
> **Marcus**

P.S. Marcus is a talented and capable person. He is also depressed. For many years he progressed as any teen and young adult from high school to college to the world of work. He is now struggling to maintain his work and independence because of depression. He feels tired, sad, and hopeless. He is unable to manufacture the energy nec-essary to accomplish his writing assignments, a task that he once loved. His job is in jeopardy and he is need of assistance.

The explanation

People with Asperger Syndrome are particularly vulnerable to mental health problems such as anxiety and depression, especially in late adolescence and early adult life (Tantam and Prestwood 1999). Depression is common in individuals with AS with about 1 in 15 people with AS experiencing such symptoms (Tantam 1991). Temple Grandin states in the video *Visual Thinking of a Person with Autism* (1999) that the most prevalent feeling experienced by adults with autism is "anxiety."

Anxiety is a common problem in people with autism and Asperger Syndrome. Muris *et al.* (1998) found that 84.1 percent of children with pervasive developmental disorder met the full criteria of at least one anxiety disorder. People with AS are apt to have anxiety resulting from constant social and environmental demands.

Depression in teens and adults with AS may be related to an increased awareness of their disability and the influence that a social disability has on social standing: isolation, loneliness, loss, a constant feeling of failure, excessive anxiety levels, dependence, past experiences with bullying and teasing, underemployment, and unemployment. Marcus is at an age where he is beginning to examine the impact of AS on his life. It is unclear whether he has become depressed because of his circumstances or if he has a biological predisposition to depression that might be present in his genetic make-up. However, at this point his depression is further complicating his life by inhibiting his ability to work and meet his writing deadlines. So, it is no longer a matter of which came first, coping or genetics, Marcus needs help.

It is important to know that people with AS can suffer from other types of mental illness including obsessive compulsive disorder, Attention Deficit Hyperactivity Disorder (ADHD), and mood swings.

The solution

Mental healthcare is the same for teens and adults with AS, as it is for NTs. The only major difference is the there is an increased likelihood that the individual with AS will experience anxiety or depression at some point in his or her life.

Good mental healthcare begins with a good evaluation. If you believe that you are suffering from any mental illness it is essential to seek a thorough evaluation by a professional trained in AS and mental illness. When searching for a practitioner to complete the evaluation it will be important for you to discover whether they have knowledge of AS and experiencing evaluating teens and adults.

To discover an experienced professional in your area you may choose to seek a referral from your physician, contact your local autism organization for a list of providers, contact your state medical association, or speak to other professionals with knowledge of autism spectrum disorders. You can then take the following steps:

1. Before calling you may want to prepare a list or script that includes everything that you need to include in your initial contact; your name, age, presenting problems, your method of payment, availability for an appointment, and what you will need to bring along on your appointment. If you decide to have someone accompany you to the appointment be sure to find out when they are available to go before you make the appointment.

2. If you call and the appointment is a long time off you may ask to be placed on a cancellation list. If someone cancels an appointment you could possibly take their place and be seen sooner. In the event that you are in crisis it is best to go straight to your local hospital emergency room.

3. After making the appointment write down the day and time of the appointment and what you are to take with you to the appointment.

4. In the event that you are diagnosed with a mental health problem there are a variety of treatment options and combinations of treatment options.

- Counseling involves meeting with a knowledgeable person who understanding your problems and who gives support, guidance, instruction, advice, and encouragement.

- Self-help groups involve meeting with other people with the same or similar problem as yours. People in the group provide each other with support, guidance, instruction, advice, and encouragement.

- Medication can only be prescribed by a physician and is useful for treating anxiety, depression, ADHD, and mood swings.

- Spiritual support provides guidance, instruction and encouragement for the individual who has chosen to embrace a belief in God.

THE TOPIC: HEALTHCARE

Healthcare is the prevention, treatment, and management of illness. Good healthcare is important for your overall well-being. Prevention of illness for teens and adults is accomplished through healthy living, refraining from risky behavior and following the guidelines outlined by physicians and dentists for routine check-ups for the purpose of early detection of illness.

Healthy living includes getting adequate nutrition, exercise, and sleep to promote wellness in addition to weight and stress management. Healthy living includes maintaining good hygiene and sanitation like washing your hands, brushing your teeth, cleaning your living area, and bathing regularly. The exact formula for healthy living depends on the individual and is highly personal. Guidelines for a healthy weight can be obtained from your healthcare provider.

Risky behaviors known to jeopardize the health of teens and adults include not wearing a seatbelt when you drive or ride in a car, not wearing a helmet when you ride a bike or motor cycle, sending a text message or using your cell phone while driving, smoking cigarettes, taking recreational drugs, drinking alcohol in excess, and driving while intoxicated. Other risky behaviors include having unprotected sex, overeating, resorting to resolving problems by using violent or aggressive solutions rather than talking though the problem, and meeting strangers from the internet without adequate screening.

Following the guidelines for routine check-ups outlined by healthcare providers including physicians and dentists is important for prevention and early detection of illness.

For teenagers it is important to get the required immunizations as determined by your physician or healthcare provider. Routine check-ups during the teen years provide the teen, parent and doctor an opportunity to discuss health concerns that sometimes arise during adolescence including obesity, dating, intercourse, sexually transmitted diseases, and stress. A typical check-up with a doctor for a teenager usually includes the following:

- measuring your height, weight, and blood pressure

- possibly blood tests to check your general health

- young men are examined for hernias and testicular cancer

- young women may receive a gynecologic exam and pap smear to check for cervical cancer and are taught how to perform a monthly breast exam, this generally occurs at age 18 years, earlier for those who are sexually active

- a general check of ears, eyes, throat and glands

- immunizations are checked and updated if needed

- vision and hearing are screened

- teeth are examined for signs of tooth decay, abnormal tooth development, dental injuries, and other oral health problems

- questions about potentially harmful behaviors and social or emotional problems.

Routine check-ups for women include measuring weight, routine physical exam, screening for breast cancer, cervical cancer, high blood pressure, diabetes, anemia, sexually transmitted diseases, immunizations, and kidney disease. Gynecological care is essential even for those who are not sexually active.

Routine check-ups for men include measuring weight, routine physical exam, high blood pressure, diabetes, cholesterol, sexually transmitted diseases, testicular exam, screening for prostrate cancer, colon cancer, and immunizations.

Dental check-ups are included on the list of important preventative routine care for teenagers and adults. Regular dental check-ups prevent tooth decay and gum disease by cleaning the teeth well, checking for and repairing cavities early, and teaching and reinforcing good oral hygiene through regular brushing, flossing and, in many areas, fluoride treatment. Good oral hygiene enhances overall health and helps teenagers and adults with self-confidence.

Medical treatment and management of illness refers to seeking treatment when ill and following through on the recommended treatments. For example when taking an antibiotic for an infection you take it just as prescribed for the correct number of days, no more-no less, or you follow a strict adherence to your diet after discovering that you have diabetes.

The challenge

If you live long enough you are bound to get sick. That's what happened to me. I am 58 and I was recently diagnosed with Type 2 diabetes. I knew that it was just a matter of time because this disease runs in my family. I have been fortunate that for all of my life my only major problem was my autism. So now I learn that my body doesn't produce enough insulin. Insulin is necessary for the body to be able to turn sugar into useful energy. Unfortunately by the time I got diagnosed I had to go on insulin injections. I have always been afraid of doctors and haven't been good about getting regular check-ups. I haven't been too good about my weight either. I'm kinda on the heavy side. I may have been able to avoid going straight to insulin shots if I had only seen the doctor sooner, oh well, maybe not. Now I am in a real dilemma because I hate shots and now I have to test my glucose every day and give myself injections. Another problem is that my diet was almost completely made up of what I am told now are bad carbohydrates, well really great carbohydrates, but just bad for me. I love bread, pasta, rice and cereal. Now I have to eat fruit, vegetables and beans. I am handling the needles better, but I really struggle with the food. So far I haven't been very successful in this area, yet.

Marvin

The explanation

An essential element to good healthcare is the management of the medical treatment for illness. This is especially important for chronic illnesses like diabetes that can be managed with good care, yet with poor care can reap havoc on the human body. Marvin is fortunate that he has access to good healthcare, his diabetes was diagnosed, and that he was provided with knowledge, medical supplies, and medicine to treat his illness. He has the knowledge that he needs to care for himself; however, his problem is not knowledge, but his ability to change his eating habits. It is unknown whether his food choices are based on sensory issues or just years of habit, but it doesn't matter, he will need to find a solution or risk serious health problems in the future.

Maintaining good health is the same for all people. It requires prevention, avoiding risks, seeking regular check-ups for prevention and early detection and managing treatment in the event of an illness. Unfortunately there are hindrances to healthcare for teens and adults with AS. These include missing knowledge, limited financial resources, poor organizational skills, general anxiety about visits to the doctor or dentist and communication difficulties. All of these factors make it difficult for the teen or adult with AS to make and keep an appointment, pay for a service, and communicate his or her needs.

The solution

The solution for managing healthcare is to gather information about prevention and the need for routine check-ups, refrain from risky behavior, identify financial resources before an emergency arises, set up an organizational system to help with your medical records, appointments, contacts and resources, a support system for remaining focused on your healthcare, and devise a system for communicating with healthcare providers.

- Knowledge can be acquired through articles in prevention health magazines, in on-line journals and from healthcare professionals.

- If you smoke you may need to think about stopping. There are smoking cessation programs that you can talk to your healthcare provider about. If you think that you drink too much seek an evaluation. Maybe you have slipped into a pattern that is unhealthy. If you are engaging in risky sexual behavior begin taking precautions. If you don't wear a seatbelt in the car start wearing it, maybe you need to wrap the strap in a soft towel for comfort. If you are active and not taking time to wear protective gear start taking the time. You are worth it!

- Financial resources can be acquired through personal health insurance, insurance through your work benefits, or through government agencies.

- An organizational system might include a file folder for medical records and a journal, notebook, daily planner, or electronic PDA for keeping track of appointments and healthcare provider contact information including name, telephone number, e-mail address, and physical address.

- The purpose of a support network is to assist you by providing encouragement to following through on the healthcare plan or commitment you have devised for yourself. A support system might include a family member, friend, colleague, or healthcare provider.

- Communicating with your healthcare provider can be accomplished best if your keep a log or journal of your general health and health habits. When you make observations or have questions write them in your journal. Take the journal with you to your appointments so that you are able to share accurate and detailed information. Without a written support people will sometimes get anxious in a doctors or dentists office and forget to tell them or ask what they need to communicate. If you tend to write a lot you will want to read over the journal before your appointment and highlight the most important information to share. Healthcare providers tend to be busy so you will need to present your concerns, observations, and questions in a summarized format.

4 Living Arrangements

In this chapter the social skills required for independent living are explored. The specific topics covered include living at home, supported living and independent living; self-care; home care, and budgeting and financial management. Each topic is defined and the purposes of each topic are presented. Personal stories are told that describe the struggle and unique challenges that teens and adults with Asperger Syndrome experience related to living arrangements. An explanation of the specific challenges presented in each scenario is presented. Practical solutions are presented in an easy-to-follow, step-by-step format to address each challenge.

THE TOPIC: LIVING AT HOME, SUPPORTED LIVING, AND INDEPENDENT LIVING

At the end of the teenage years or the beginning of the adult years it is natural for an individual to leave the family home to a home of his or her own. It is important to recognize that there is no single correct living arrangement for everyone and for this reason not everyone will elect to leave the family home. For people who want a change, a variety of options are available.

Adults can choose from a variety of living arrangements based upon their preference, level of self-care and resources. Living options may include:

- rented apartment, condominium, townhouse, or house

- purchased condominium, townhouse, or house

- supported accommodation

- group home

- with family.

A rented property is leased from an owner or company. A renter is usually responsible for a monthly fee and some utilities. A renter is generally not responsible to pay the property taxes. A one-month security deposit is generally required at the time of the lease in addition to the first month's rent. Sometimes people choose to rent a property with one or two other people to reduce the cost. The responsibilities of a renter include the following:

- Paying your rent and utilities on time.

- Reporting any damage or problems when they happen.

- Keeping the noise to a reasonable level.

- Taking care of the property and keeping it clean.

- Preventing illegal activities from going on in your house.

When renting it is important to know that you can be evicted from your property under certain conditions: not paying your rent, damaging the property or allowing someone else to damage the property, engaging in antisocial behavior like being noisy and getting into arguments with your neighbors or the landlord.

Purchasing a home can be nice if you have the resources. To purchase a home the buyer is required to have a regular income at a level that can support the purchase. A home owner is responsible for all of the expenses and costs for the mortgage, taxes, and upkeep of the property.

Supported accommodation is a living arrangement that allows an adult to live independently with support services generally provided by an agency or nonprofit organization. The services increase the likelihood that an adult with special needs will be successful. Support services might include social services, financial services, housekeeping, assistance with self-care, and emotional support.

A group home is a living arrangement that allows several adults to live together in a single dwelling with a care giver on-site 24 hours a day. This setting allows adults with more significant disabilities to live in their own home with around the clock support and services.

Living at home with family is the living arrangement for the majority of adults with autism and AS. According to a recent study in the United States, 9 percent of the adults with AS live with a married partner or on their own, 23 percent live independently with some support, 2 percent live in a group home and 66 percent live with their parents (Geller and Cavanagh 2005). Living with parents provides familiarity and social contact without the cost of independent living. As parents age this is a concern for the many who reside in the family home.

The challenge

> I live in an apartment near the community college I attend. I am taking two classes right now, computer programming and communications. I like living in my apartment because it gives me a chance to do what I want and hang-out with my friend John. John has an apartment on the third floor in my building. We get together to play computer games and sometimes we go to a movie. My apartment is small, but it is good for just one person. I have a caseworker and she comes by every week to check on me. When she comes over we work on things like cooking and balancing my checkbook. She already taught me how to clean my apartment and do my

laundry, although my mom usually takes my laundry home with her and brings back clean clothes. I like having my own place, it is pretty cool!

Dustin

The explanation

It is natural and expected in most communities for a young adult to move out of his or her parent's home into a place of their own. It is complicated and expensive for young adults to move into their own place, but most figure out how to accomplish this by working several jobs, learning a profession that pays well enough, or getting a few roommates to share expenses. Many young people marry and with combined incomes and shared costs having their own place is possible. It is not that easy for people with AS to find suitable housing as adults. Hindrances to locating appropriate housing are many including the lack of affordable housing, underemployment, and unemployment.

There is shortage of affordable housing in many communities. People without disabilities can share expenses with roommates or relocate to surrounding areas where the cost of housing is more accommodating. It is more difficult for a person with a disability to find a suitable roommate and it is much harder to relocate since this involves leaving your support system and may require driving an automobile, which may not be possible depending on the severity of a person's disability.

Insufficient income is another huge problem because adults with AS are typically underemployed. Underemployment refers to a situation in which a worker is employed but not in the desired capacity, whether in terms of compensation, hours, or level of skill and experience. According to a recent study in the U.S. an adult on the autism spectrum with a bachelor's degree earns on an average $19,750 compared to $49,050 average earnings for NTs. The figures are more dismal for the teen or adult with only a high school diploma. An adult on the autism spectrum with a high school diploma earns on the average $1,267 compared to $25,487 average earnings for NTs (Geller and Cavanagh 2005).

Unemployment is another major problem. In the U.K. 6 percent of the adults on the autism spectrum are employed full-time and only 12 percent of individual with AS are employed full-time (Barnard *et al.* 2001). The figures are consistent in the United States.

Support services for teens and adults with AS are limited. In Dustin's situation he is fortunate to live in a community that has supportive housing for adults with AS. He is able to live alone in a small apartment in a building where other young adults with AS also live. The apartment is within walking distance of a community college, shopping, restaurants, and other recreational activities. His mother remains involved in his life, but no longer has full responsibly for his care. He now cares for himself with some assistance.

The solution

Living arrangements are highly personal and depend greatly upon your preferences, interests, abilities, and resources. You will need to carefully research the housing options in your community.

Decide which living arrangement suits you best. Completing the "Living Arrangements" survey in My Journal on page 190 will help you in this process. You can then design a plan to maximize your independence. Independence is taking care of yourself and your surroundings. Independence is possible in any living arrangement. It depends on how you choose to conduct yourself.

Whether living with family, in a group home, or on your own, you need to be able to do the following:

- Contribute financially from your earnings or assistance.

- Care for yourself and your belongings.

- Complete tasks of cleaning, straightening, and caring for the property.

- Conduct yourself as you would if you were in any other living arrangement, with dignity for yourself and respect for others.

Look for resources in your community to assist with your housing selection. Government agencies, schools, adult organizations and nonprofit organizations, are good places to start. Resources are limited so it would be good for parents of teens to begin this search as early as possible. Sometimes the waiting lists for services can be many years.

THE TOPIC: SELF-CARE

Self-care generally refers to an individual's ability to care for his or her overall health and well-being including nutrition, fitness, mental health, and healthcare. Since these topics are covered in length in other sections of the book this section will be dedicated to hygiene and grooming as it applies to good health and self-confidence.

Hygiene refers to the sanitary care of the body, which means keeping the body clean and free from dirt. Hygiene involves bathing, shampooing, skincare, nail care, oral care, and applying products to inhibit the growth of bacteria as in the case of deodorant. The frequency of bathing and shampooing depends upon the expectations within a culture. Some groups of people believe that bathing daily is essential while others view bathing a couple of times a week as sufficient.

Most people recognize that germs travel through touch so frequent hand washing is generally expected as a common form of hygiene. Keeping fingernails free from dirt is also a sanitary expectation in most places. Acne and other skin sores have various causes, but are all fueled by staph bacteria. Staph is spread by touch so frequent hand washing and nail care is important to keep the body sanitary and healthy.

Grooming in the animal world involves removing dirt and parasites from the fur, skin, or features. For humans grooming refers to the tasks and routines that keep our appearance neat. Grooming that denotes a neat appearance differs by culture. Some groups of people view a man as well-groomed if he shaves his beard everyday, while others define a well-groomed man as one who never shaves, but only shapes his beard. Grooming includes anything that involves a person's appearance hair, beard, nails, skin, and make-up, the shape of the body, clothing, shoes, and accessories.

Being part of a society has benefits. Those benefits include employment, protection, and membership, but it also has requirements. The requirements for living in a society include working hard and contributing to the betterment of the society, abiding by the laws and rules so that people are safe, and fitting in the best that you can by conforming in conduct and appearance. Even people who find themselves on the fringe of society because of disability can benefit by conforming to the requirements of the group in the best way that they can. Each person will have to observe the requirement of his or her society to determine which features of appearance require grooming to be considered neat and trim, or well-groomed.

The challenge

I have always been a rather plain person. I am most comfortable wearing jeans with a stretchy waist and a large flannel shirt. I wear my hair very short because it is easier to take care of and I never wear make-up. I met my sister for lunch last week at a restaurant near my house. We ordered our food, but before it came I went to the ladies room. When I got to the door a lady was coming out and she was startled. She nicely told me, "Sorry sir, the men's room is over there." I said, "I am a lady." She was startled again and apologized. I think that she could tell from my voice that I was a girl. I didn't get upset because this has happened a few times before. I guess I just don't fit in anywhere.

Stephanie

The explanation

Hygiene is important for health and grooming is important for belonging. Hygiene and grooming are culturally determined. To detect the hygienic and grooming expectations for a specific culture an individual needs to be able to observe their surroundings, recognize the interrelatedness of people, embrace the culture and recognize the value of certain forms of conformity related to appearance.

For the teen and adult with AS conforming to hygienic and grooming expectations may be problematic for a variety of reasons. Many individuals with AS have struggled much of their lives to "fit-in" or be included by their culture without success. To ask those individuals to embrace the grooming traditions of this culture is hard to accept. Others may not really comprehend the purpose of conformity of appearance and its relevance or benefit for them. Others do not know how or where to get good grooming advice, while others do not have the resources to afford grooming services. For others grooming and hygienic habits are dictated by their sensory systems.

In Stephanie's story her sensory system has pretty much dictated the clothes that she will wear. She is only comfortable in jeans with an elastic waist and flannel shirt. She wears her hair short for ease and does not wear make-up because it isn't anything that she has ever wanted to do. She isn't trying to look like a man, but she isn't grooming herself as a woman might in her culture. While it appears that she has accepted herself, the tone of her comments leads the reader to think that she is more resigned than accepting.

The solution

Grooming choices are highly personal and culturally bound so in this section of the book the guidelines will focus on observation, reflection, and analysis rather than specific rules for hygiene and grooming.

- Observe your surroundings to identify whether the culture in which you live holds hygiene in high regard. Complete

"Hygiene and Grooming" in My Journal on page 191 to guide your observations, reflection, and analysis.

- For cultures that hold hygiene and grooming in high regard, not adhering to the cultural standard will have a cost. If you do not adhere to the hygiene and grooming norm what do you think the cost is for you?

- Observe your surroundings to identify the perimeters that your culture uses to decide whether a person is considered well-groomed or not.

- From your observations, reflections, and analysis are you satisfied with your appearance or are there changes that you would like to make?

- Sensitivities to touch, fragrances and noise can inhibit a person's desire to have a haircut or apply lotions and cosmetics. Complete "Sensory Challenges" in My Journal on page 192. Allow this to guide your observations, reflections and analysis regarding physical sensitivities that might interfere with good grooming and hygiene practices.

THE TOPIC: HOME CARE

Home care refers to the overall organization, care, and management of the home. Home care includes a range of tasks: selecting furnishings, organizing belongings, straightening, house cleaning, laundry, small repairs, and cooking. The purpose of home care is to provide a safe, clean, and pleasant environment to live. Learning how to care for a home requires training and practice. Training includes strategies for selecting and gathering furnishings that will make your home comfortable, strategies for organizing the environment so that your belongings are stored for easy access, procedures for house cleaning that support the best sanitation, practices for laundry that clean and protect your clothes, and procedures for cooking that are safe and hygenic and give you good tasty food. Practicing good home care can improve organizational skills and the overall quality of life.

The challenge

The biggest challenge in our household is getting to events on time and with all of the required items. I spend an enormous amount of time looking for things. I work from home and my wife works in an office. It is my responsibility to get our two children off to school in the morning. Everyday it is something, a missing shoe, toothbrush, favorite toy, book bag, hair tie, and even an occasional coat. I can't keep track of socks at all, forget it. It is really bad on library book return day. We can never find the books. It is so frustrating.

Daniel

The explanation

As a child many of us thought that our parents were punishing us because they made us perform household chores that included picking-up after ourselves. It turns out that this wasn't punishment at all, but needed teaching and practice that would keep us from punishing ourselves later in life. Keeping a clean, comfortable, and organized home is good for your health and well-being. It can help save money since you will not have to regularly replace missing items and the saved time will help increase your productivity.

In Daniel's story he relives the same problem every day, not because he is foolish, but because he is disorganized. Disorganization is a prevalent characteristic in many teens and adults with AS. He is a caring father who wants his children to attend school and he wants them to fit-in. He sees his problem as a finding problem when it is really an attention problem. If Daniel were more attentive to organizing the home so that every belonging has a place and he teaches and reinforces his children to put their things in the designated place he will no longer have a finding problem. This takes an enormous amount of effort on the front end, but can reap rewards like more time on your hands and happier relationships.

The solution

Home care begins with observing your surroundings. It then requires study and practice as does any other set of capabilities.

- When moving into a new home, take time to organize the space for maximum use and enjoyment. You will most likely need to gather furnishings unless they are provided. Remember that fewer items require less organizing, straightening, cleaning, and care. Complete the "Home Furnishings" survey in My Journal on page 193 to determine which furnishings you will need to set up your home.

- Systems and routines for organizing your home are essential to good home care. Providing a spot for each item will help you keep track of your belongings, will reduce frustration, will save your money and will enhance your productivity.

- Proper house cleaning and laundry procedures can lengthen the life of your belongings, save you money, and enhance the quality of life. These procedures can be learned through a variety of sources: family members, friends, agencies, on-line experts, magazine articles, and books.

- Cooking can provide more than tasty food, it can provide interest, a creative outlet, and enjoyment in life. The skills for cooking can be learned through a variety of sources: family members, friends, by taking courses, on-line experts, magazine articles, and books.

- Seeking guidance and instruction in home care may require interaction with other people, many of which would be considered acquaintances. For these interactions you may want to prepare a list or script of your observations and needs before approaching the person to facilitate the exchange, allowing you to gather the information you need to go forward in managing your home.

THE TOPIC: BUDGETING AND FINANCIAL MANAGEMENT

Managing finances involve budgeting, banking, and investments. Of these skills budgeting can be the most important and challenging. Without a good solid budget there is rarely enough money to worry about banking and investments. Budgeting involves managing money by having a spending plan, using credit wisely and building up savings (Consumer Credit Counseling Services 2003).

Budgeting is important for all levels of income, for the teenager who receives an allowance or small paycheck for part-time work and the adult who receives assistance or a large salary. Managing money wisely will produce benefits.

The challenge

> I work for a nonprofit organization so my salary is less than it might be if I were working in the public sector. I have no intention of changing jobs, but I have to live on a tight budget. I share an apartment with a colleague so the costs are not as bad as they might be for our part of town. I never had a class on financial management or budgeting. I had never written a check until I was 25. Before then I really didn't have any money and I still don't have very much. I like living on my own and I want it to stay that way so budgeting my money is extremely important. I have no debt and no credit cards. I try to pay cash

for everything. My budget basically consists of just not spending money. I generally eat at home except when I pack and carry my lunch to work. I turn off the lights when I leave a room and I only run the clothes washer and dishwasher when they are full. I take a shower instead of a bath and when I must buy something I shop at the discount stores with coupons. I eat a lot of rice and pasta because this is cheap food and I am careful to only buy as many fruits and vegetables that I can eat before they spoil. I have enough money to get by, but this is a stressful way to live.

Margie

The explanation

Managing money is much more than just not spending. People work so that they can live and enjoy the benefits of their hard labor. In Margie's story she has learned to minimize her expenses, but this level of frugal living may not be necessary and it is certainly stressful. Margie needs a spending plan. A spending plan is your plan for spending your money.

The solution

A spending plan is designed by looking at your income and deciding how you will spend that money.

- Financial advisors typically recommend that you begin by paying a small amount of money to yourself in a savings account. This money can be used for unexpected emergencies. Unexpected emergencies frequently force people to use credit unwisely. Credit card debt can greatly inhibit your financial freedom.

- Decide what expenses are most important to you. In Margie's situation she would say that the expense of her shared apartment is the most important. To help facilitate your planning complete "Personal Spending Plan" worksheet in My Journal on page 194.

- If you need assistance with the spending plan or any area of money management it would be good to contact a free consumer credit counseling service. They are typically available by telephone, on-line, and for in-person appointments. Your contact will be with an acquaintance so it would help for you to complete a list or script outlining your needs before making the contact.

5   Education,
       Training,
       and Employment

In this chapter the communication skills required for employment are explored. The specific topics covered include career and vocational assessment; college, technical institutes and apprenticeships; finding employment; and keeping a job. Each topic is defined and the purposes of each topic are presented. Personal stories are told that describe the struggle and unique challenges that teens and adults with Asperger Syndrome experience related to education, training, and employment. An explanation follows each scenario. Practical solutions are presented in an easy-to-follow, step-by-step format.

THE TOPIC: CAREER AND VOCATIONAL ASSESSMENT

Meaningful employment is too important to be left to chance. Careful planning and educational programming is essential to achieving this goal. Career and vocational assessments are two tools that can assist in this planning.

Career assessment refers to the process of gathering information about you for the purpose of matching your interests and personality traits to an occupation or profession. Professions are occupations that typically require special training that generally leads to a lifework.

Special training can be time consuming and costly. For these reasons it is useful to seek guidance through a career assessment.

Career assessments typically involve the use of self-reporting surveys, tests and checklists. The majority of assessment tools rely upon self-reporting by the person having the assessment. In order for the assessment to be valid and useful, the reporting must be truthful and accurate. Self-report survey tools generally require reading and responding to a wide variety of questions about your interests and preferences. If a person struggles in reading, the assessment tool can be read aloud by another person, allowing the individual to mark her response unless, of course, the purpose of the test is to evaluate reading skills. Career assessments can be accessed through employment agencies, government agencies, colleges and universities, and through private businesses.

Vocational assessment refers to the process of gathering information about an individual for the purpose of determining vocational preference and potential in an occupational trade. Vocational assessment may include observations, anecdotal information from people like teachers who know you, on-the-job try-outs, surveys, checklists, tests, and work samples. A vocational assessment is concerned with gathering information in the following areas:

- career awareness

- personal interests

- aptitudes

- special needs: accommodations if needed

- learning style(s)

- work habits and behaviors

- personal and social skills

- values and attitudes towards work

- self-concept
- work tolerances.

Through the assessment process, the individual increases in self-awareness and develops a better understanding of his skills. For many people, participating in a vocational assessment has also increased their interest in work and prompted other interesting changes. Some individuals have increased their interest in discussing their vocational or career futures. Specific vocational education plans may develop realistic career interests, an increased interest in school work, and more self-confidence and/or self-esteem (Vocational Assessment 1990).

The benefits of vocational assessment for students with disabilities were outlined by the National Information Center for Children and Youth with Disabilities in 1990:

> Active participation of students in the assessment process can be an important factor in showing them how school connects to the outside world of work and in motivating them in their school work. Moreover, through the assessment process, students and families have the opportunity to gather information about various careers. Learning about various jobs, trying out work roles, exploring interests, and getting feedback on many different aspects of individual abilities and performance broaden students' knowledge base of the work-world and themselves. This allows them to explore what careers might be appropriate for them and to identify those that are not. (Vocational Assessment 1990, p.3)

These same benefits are essentials for all individuals. It is never too late to seek an evaluation that will assist in identifying the occupation for which you are best suited. Temple Grandin (Grandin and Barron 2005, p.26) stated:

> I have observed that the high-functioning people with autism or Asperger who make the best adjustments in life are the

ones who have satisfying jobs… Conversely, the most unhappy people on the spectrum I have met are those who did not develop a good, employable skill or a hobby that they can share with others. With so much of adult life spent in our jobs, it makes sense that people with satisfying jobs will be generally happier and able to respond better to the different situations that arise.

The challenge

My vocational testing tells me that I have really strong strengths and very weak weaknesses. The testing matched me to my current job. My strengths are in numbers. I can remember the telephone number, birth date, and license plate number for everyone I have ever met. I like any activity with numbers. My entire high school work experience was in the public library where my job was to reshelf the books. I love that job! I am also very good at that job. I also like to sort and straighten things so my mom tells me that I am very good to have around the library. My weaknesses are that I don't have a lot of energy, I'm a little weak and I struggle when people get too close. I am going through transition because I will graduate from high school next year. I really would like to continue working at the library. They know me pretty well now and it is going pretty good. I think that this would be a pretty good job for me.

Max

P.S. Max has autism. He is enrolled in a life skills community job program through his high school. He started working at the local public library two years ago for four hours a week and has over the last two years increased that time to 15 hours each week. He sorts and shelves the library books in addition to some other straightening duties. He is currently learning to dust and use a push sweeper to tidy the library. He is accurate, reliable, but works slowly. The library does not have the funds to hire him after high school, although they are trying to make some arrangements to keep him on for about 12 hours a week after graduation.

The explanation

Career and vocational assessment is useful in matching an individual to a vocational or career choice that he or she may be best suited to. In Max's situation it was hard for his parents and teachers to identify a particular job placement because his strong interests were so narrow, but the vocational testing clearly identified a variety of different skills related to number sequences and memory. This information was useful in matching Max to a suitable job. The vocational assessment and job experience has increased Max's interest in work. He wants to work and it hopeful that he will be able to keep his job. Another benefit of the assessment was bringing the entire Individual Education Program (IEP) team together with the vocational and career assessment expert for planning.

The solution

Career and vocational assessment are often available to students while they are attending public school, but that is only a small part of the community of teens and adults with AS. For those out of school, seeking an assessment will be a little more challenging, nevertheless important.

1. As with any other change the first step is to observe, reflect, analyze, and evaluate your current situation. You may choose to answer the following questions about your current employment situation.

    ° Do you want to work?

    ° Are you having trouble finding employment?

    ° Is your current work satisfying?

    ◦ Does your work provide you with the necessary financial support?

    ◦ Would you rather be doing something else?

    ◦ Could you benefit from a vocational or career assessment?

2.   Career and vocational assessments can be taken through government agencies serving teens and adults with disabilities, employment agencies, colleges and universities, and nonprofit organizations. Many of these sources are accessible on-line under the heading vocational and career assessment.

3.   Before making your initial contact it would be useful for you to record your questions and comments in list or script form. It could also be helpful, as with any search, to enlist the help of family or friends. Sometimes sorting through the various offerings can be frustrating and time consuming.

THE TOPIC: COLLEGE, TECHNICAL INSTITUTES, AND APPRENTICESHIPS

Colleges and universities, technical institutes, and apprenticeships provide teens and adults with the knowledge, skills, and capabilities they need to enter the work force. Making a decision to choose any of these programs will depend greatly upon your interests, aptitude, and resources.

Colleges and universities offer a wide variety of opportunities to students. Many colleges and universities offer a liberal arts education which is aimed at building general knowledge and intellectual capabilities, while others focus predominantly on applied programs that spend the majority of time on skill sets related to a specific profession. Still others are a balance between liberal arts and applied programs. Many professions require diplomas from colleges or universities in addition to graduate or professional school preparation.

Technical and vocational institutes generally offer coursework and extensive apprenticeships that focus on the specific capabilities required for a given trade. Some programs require licensure while others do not. Technical institutes offer programs that range from plumbing to assisting a dentist. Technical and vocational programs in general cost less than colleges and universities and the programs are designed to be completed in less time.

Apprenticeships provide work-based training to teens and adults who want to learn vocational skills and gain qualifications while working. An apprenticeship involves locating a qualified and experienced person working in an occupation of interest who is willing to provide instruction and guidance in the chosen occupation.

The challenge

If I were to summarize my college experience thus far in a single word, it would be "trying." I say this because although I am disabled, I do not believe myself incapable of my workload; quite the contrary actually. However, for reasons I cannot fully explain and due to barriers I cannot precisely identify, I find an ever-present additional gravity added to my course load. My anxieties lead me to treat featherweight assignments as though they were anvils.

Coming to college and staying there is easily one of the most difficult ordeals with which I have ever had to cope. I am a homebody and have rarely ventured far from the house in which I grew up. Taking up residence in my single room at college was a transition for which I could not have fully prepared myself. Surrounded by strange people and denied the familiarity of my home, I withdrew from my surroundings. Instead of acclimating to campus life, I retreated inwardly and immersed myself in a sea of fear, anxiety, and doubt.

Sleep, or lack of it, was another issue. Most nights I would be unable to fall asleep, staying awake until three or four in the morning. Rest could only be achieved when my exhaustion grew too great to bear. In the morning, I forced myself awake at seven (or eight or bountiful nine, depending on how poorly I was faring), utilizing the campus' caffeine reserves to help me maintain consciousness.

My nerves got so bad that I was unable to focus on my workload. Anxiety rendered me mentally immobile and it was not until hours or worse yet, minutes before classes began that my fear of failure would override my paralysis, so that I could finally get moving.

I visited the college counseling center and they told me that sooner or later my unhealthy lifestyle would cause my grades to flounder and force me to improve or flunk out. Unfortunately this never happened. The conflict would not be resolved so easily. My personal habits continually declined, yet I maintained mostly commendable grades all year. For me, the problem of school is not a failure to succeed academically, but an inability to exist comfortably. Make no mistake, my work ethic faltered badly when I began my college career. My grades are acceptable; however, I consider the quality of my work far below that which I find tolerable.

I want to say that the resources afforded me at college have been exceptional. I have no complaints about my accommodations or the personnel who provide them. My difficulties on campus are almost entirely internally driven and, as such, treatment must also stem from within. My college is a genuinely friendly campus and about as unthreatening an environment as I could hope to find in a school. I can think of no satisfactory reason why I must struggle so much to achieve anything.

As my situation currently stands, I am forced to make regular trips home on weekends to find the peace of mind necessary to recharge and begin anew each week. I intentionally applied only to schools within an hour's drive of home, suspecting I might need the respite. I am at my peak ability on Monday morning. Returning fresh from home, I am able to focus, study and achieve more than I can at any other point in the week. By Friday, I am reaching my limits and usually find any sustained thought difficult. Going from week to week in this manner is an incredibly draining process. I probably would have given up on college entirely, were it not for the occasional glimmers of hope that shine through.

I am improving. Although my problems remain, I am finding it slowly but progressively easier to maintain my composure. I have always striven to make sure that, while my anxieties may impinge upon my ambitions, I will not allow mere angst total victory over my will. I try to stay active on campus. If I can ground myself in an activity, it helps to keep my self-doubts at bay. To date I have appeared in two of my college's theatrical productions, maintained my membership in the Honors program and am currently writing for the campus newspaper as well as its yearbook.

I do not know quite where my experiences at college thus far are leading. I have no intentions of abandoning the school or my dreams. However I do lament that both can be so difficult to hold onto. For now, my strategy remains the same. As long as I can get up in the morning, I can make it through a new day.

Steven

The explanation
Getting into a college or university program, technical institute or even an apprenticeship may not be the most difficult part of the

process; the part that may turn out to be the most difficult could be staying and completing the program.

For Steven adjusting to college life was hard. He refers to himself as a homebody and even through he has the privacy of a single room at college the fact that it isn't home is highly stressful. His ability to cope was challenged by worsening anxiety that was further exasperated by sleep deprivation and vice versa. He thought that living away from home might be stressful so he selected a college just an hour's drive from home. He discovered that spending every weekend at home refreshes his strength for the next week. He is meeting with success but wishes that it didn't have to be so hard.

The solution

Plan, plan, plan is the solution for attending any type of post-secondary education.

1. Before searching for any post-secondary setting take time to observe and reflect upon your needs. Try to envision yourself living away from home, what does it look like? Do you see yourself living away at college, university or trade school, or would you rather attend a program close to your family home? If you live away from your family home, do you see yourself needing a private or shared room? Whether you live at home or at school, do you see yourself taking fewer courses over a longer period of time? Are you in need of a support system at school from the time that you arrive? Are you able to seek and ask for help? Are you able to tell others about your disability? Are your sensory needs significant enough to warrant accommodations? Are your learning needs significant enough to warrant accommodations? To facilitate your reflection on these questions complete the "Planning for Post-secondary Education Worksheet" on p.196

2. Identify a list of potential institutions you would like to visit. Make an appointment with the disabilities

coordinator of the school for the day of your visit. Be sure to identify the records that you will need to provide to receive support from disability services. It is easier to not use services that are already in place, than to get services when an emergency arises.

3. Using the information from your personal reflection and the information from the school make your decision. Be sure that the accommodations you need are agreed upon and will be in place from your first day at school.
    Accommodations might include:

    ° a single room

    ° a mentor for residential life

    ° support group opportunities from the counseling center or disabilities service office

    ° crisis plan

    ° tutoring services

    ° writing lab services

    ° faculty in-service on appropriate pedagogy for learners with AS

    ° classroom accommodations, as needed: extended times for tests; increased professor availability and a structured classroom setting.

4. Maintain regular contact with the disabilities coordinator. Meet other students with similar needs to provide each other with support. As you progress through the years try helping new students as they come to the institute. It is amazing to see how helping others can help you.

5. Get involved in activities and attend events on campus that are of personal interest. Involvement in preferred activities can be enjoyable and distracting in a positive way.

THE TOPIC: FINDING EMPLOYMENT

Employment refers to having a job that provides the funds to buy the things needed to live. Employment provides people with meaning, purpose, and satisfaction in life.

In order to secure a job an individual must possess knowledge, skills, or capabilities that someone else wants or needs and is willing to pay for. Knowledge, skills, and capabilities can be learned and developed in a number of different ways. Some people choose to go to college, trade or technical schools; others choose an apprenticeship, while others choose to get a job at an entry level position that requires few skills and increase their skills over time.

Before being hired an individual must be able to demonstrate to the prospective employer that he or she possesses certain knowledge, skills, or capabilities. This occurs in many different ways; for professional positions a college diploma, professional license, or certificate along with references from people who are familiar with the quality of your work is typically sufficient to demonstrate your capabilities. For skilled and unskilled positions longevity in a previous job along with good references signal a prospective employer that you have skills and capabilities. For someone entering the work force without any experience or marketable skills it can be difficult.

The challenge

> I am an artist and have a strong portfolio. I freelance because this is what works best for me. I like the freedom that comes from choosing my own work schedule, although it has not been without problems. For the first few years in this role it was either feast or famine. If I was hired I did well and my earnings were excellent, but I didn't always get the job. I couldn't seem to get past the interviewers. I have AS. I have enormous difficulty interpreting nonverbal cues, I'm awkward, eye contact is painful, and my affect is low and flat. I just don't interview

well. Things turned around when I figured out how to market my skills and not my personality.

Janice

P.S. Janice is an accomplished artist. She has chosen to work as a free-lance artist because that extends the flexibility that she needs to live. A major drawback to this type of work is that jobs start and stop. When they stop she has to find a new job. She worked within the traditional application-interview model until she discovered that she needed to market her skills and not her personality. With the help from friends with technical skills she has been able to create an amazing digital portfolio that highlights her strengths and minimizes her weaknesses. She also includes in the portfolio a self-disclosure statement that is almost like a short motion picture. This is her way to help the prospective employer "think in autism" (Betts and Patrick 2006). Her approach was warmly received.

The explanation

The employment rate for adults with disabilities is well below that for adults without disabilities in every country in the world. This places the adult with a disability at a tremendous disadvantage of finding full-time employment, but the situation is not impossible. For many people like Janice it will require thinking outside of the box, in other words problem solving in a nontraditional way.

Janice decided early in her adult life that she was not able to work in a traditional setting and would be better suited for contract work. She developed her personal talent in art into a marketable product. It took her a little longer to realize that she needed to approach potential clients in a nontraditional way as well. She discovered that by providing potential clients with an electronic portfolio of her work along with information on her disability that the number of contracts increased.

The solution

Finding work in a limited market requires planning. You will have to be creative and think outside of the box.

1. Identify your interests and talents. A vocational and career assessment could assist in this process.

2. Select ways to increase your knowledge, learn new skills, and develop the capabilities associated with your strengths and interests. It is possible to do this through self-study and on-line courses if travel is a problem.

3. Identify products and/or services that you could provide to others that are connected to your knowledge and skill set.

4. Identify ways to market your knowledge and skills. You could work as an entrepreneur for yourself or for someone else. If you choose to work in a traditional setting, having a good understanding of your knowledge and skills will enhance your chances of being hired.

5. If a nontraditional setting appeals more to you investigate other forms of service and product delivery through the internet or postal services.

THE TOPIC: KEEPING A JOB

"Keeping a job" refers to continuous employment in a position where you want to remain. Remaining employed has many benefits. These benefits include seniority, increased opportunities for promotions and raises in salary, familiarity with the work, the setting and the people, increased financial security, and not having to search for new employment.

Remaining employed requires capabilities that go beyond the specific skills required for the actual job you are performing. These capabilities include your work habits, values, interpersonal skills, ethics, and productivity. Specific rules and requirements will differ depending upon your occupation and community, but there are general expectations that apply to most situations.

Employers want their employees to have good work habits. "Work habits" refers to the way that you behave while on the job. Some of the most important work habits include punctuality, good attendance, refraining from profane or obscene language, attending to detail, good conduct, and keeping your mind on your work. Poor work habits include tardiness, absenteeism, aggressive behavior and language, poor productivity, and poor interpersonal behaviors. Poor work will lead to dismissal.

"Values" refers to the attitudes, beliefs and customs that people hold in high regard. They are often the foundation on which people make decisions. While we often think of values as personal and private it's important to point out that values exist in the workplace. Values in the workplace might include your employers desire to see creativity, independence, your interest in achievement, and prestige, cleanliness, your positive contributions to the work environment, your willingness to accept supervision. Places of employment have established values on which they make decisions, including hiring and firing of employees.

Any time people are together, there is a chance that there will be conflict related to values. Employers will have some sensitivity to the differences between people in this area, but ongoing conflict related to differing values may lead to poor interpersonal relationships that provoke dismissal. In order to remain employed it is important to identify the values of your company and adhere to those as you are able.

"Interpersonal skills" in the workplace refer to your ability to get along with your supervisor, peers, and subordinates. At work, employees are generally expected to maintain a submissive attitude towards their supervisor. They are expected to be friendly and cooperative towards their peers, and they are to be helpful, fair, kind, and firm with their subordinates.

"Ethics" refers to a person's beliefs and attitudes about right and wrong. Ethical behavior is the way that we behave based upon what we believe. Ethics are personal and corporate. Examples of ethics in the workplace include beliefs related to honesty, fairness, justice, helping, the value of others, and the value of work.

"Productivity" measures whether you perform and produce at a rate that is average or better for your occupation, or consistently perform and produce in line with the agreed-upon expectations. In some settings "productivity" refers to the manufacturing of a specific number of items, in others the total number of sales, while in others the degree and level of creativity. Productivity varies considerably between occupations. This is an expectation that needs to be established early and clarified frequently in the working relationship since this is often a reason given for dismissal.

The challenge

> I started working on this job three months ago. I just got my first employee evaluation and it is not very good. At this company I will need to get at least a satisfactory evaluation to be hired on permanently. I really need this job because I have just about burned all of my bridges. The evaluation says that I am not a good team player and that my appearance is "not neat." I have never been on a team and generally prefer to work alone. Other people tend to hold me back. As for my appearance I think that I look just fine. Before this job I was unemployed for six months so I don't have the money to buy a new suit. As for my appearance I do the best that I can with what I have. Besides, this is my way to express myself.
>
> **Taylor**

The explanation

Many teens and adults with AS are unemployed or underemployed. This means that they are jobless or are in a position that is below their capabilities, are working fewer hours than others or are being paid less. The reasons for unemployment and underemployment certainly differ between individuals, but tend to be related to work habits, interpersonal struggles, or productivity.

As stated earlier in the book individuals with AS tend to be honest and like routine. Honesty and an adherence to routine can be good work habits; however, it gets complicated because not all workplaces want someone who holds tightly or rigidly to his or her ethics. Holding tightly to ethics can lead some people to be viewed as potential problems because they might report something that others do not want reported, they may be "whistle blowers."

Poor attention to task, poor organizational skills, and sensory issues can inhibit productivity, which can be interpreted by an employer as poor work habits, rather than a personal hurdle. A lack of understanding by employers can cause dismissal. The single most effective strategy for preventing misunderstandings in any of the areas described is to provide the employer with information. As an individual with a disability self-disclosure can go a long way in building understanding and alliance with your employer that could protect you from dismissal when problems arise.

The solution

Being proactive in your area of employment is important. Proactive measures might include self-disclosure of your disability to your employers, along with a request for specific accommodations to be provided by your employer that will increase the likelihood that you successfully acclimate to your job and be productive, as long as the accommodations are viewed as reasonable by your employer and of course that depends on your occupation and where you work.

You want your employer to learn to "think in autism" (Betts and Patrick 2006). This means that you want your employer to begin to see the world from your perspective. When this happens there are far fewer misunderstandings and those misunderstandings that do occur are cleared up more rapidly.

Work related accommodations could include:

- Assistive technology (AT) selected specifically for you in the job that you are performing. The cost is generally minor, yet the benefits can be huge. Read more about the use of AT for teens and adults with AS in Chapter 6: Adaptive Tools.

- A job coach or mentor who would be accessible to you to ask questions and discuss concerns without fear of retaliation. They could provide additional insight, guidance, and encouragement in the areas of communication and interpersonal relationships.

- A plan for handling conflicts with co-workers if they arise.

- A set of secret signals that could be used to notify your supervisor, mentor, and/or colleagues that you need a break.

- An overall accommodation plan that would be written and revised as needed.

6   Adaptive Tools

In this chapter the adaptive tools referenced in the book are described in greater detail. The specific tools include assistive technology, direct instruction, effective listening, eye gaze, fix-up strategies, lists, note-taking, role-playing, scripts, self-assessment, self-determination, and self-disclosure.

ASSISTIVE TECHNOLOGY

Assistive technology (AT) is a generic term for a variety of devices that enable people with disabilities to be more independent, productive, and successful in the areas of personal care, independent living, socialization, organization, education, and work.

AT can be grouped into three categories: low-tech, mid-tech, and high-tech. Low-tech devices are generally easy to use, inexpensive to purchase, widely available, and involve little or no training. Mid-tech devices are somewhat more complex, often requiring a battery. High-tech devices tend to be more costly and frequently require some training.

Low-tech devices for the person with AS:

- Sticky notes and removable highlighter tape can be used to mark important word or sections in a text.

- Pencil grip can help with fine motor writing difficulties.

- Graph paper or paper grids made on a computer help to align numbers when you're doing mathematical computations.

- Communication books with words, symbols, or pictures representing frequently used messages can help you communicate verbally or nonverbally in new or anxious situations.

- Timers can be used to show how much time an activity will take, helping you to pace yourself through the activity.

- Seat cushions or carefully selected chairs can help with the posture needed to use your arms and hands effectively. They can also help with attention, by providing a calming effect.

- A personalized sensory kit that includes items that soothe the individual. Suggestions might include: a thick rubber band, a Velcro strip, a stress ball, hard lemon candies, hand lotion (scented or not), modeling clay, chewing gum, ear-plugs, or headphones.

Mid-tech devices for a person with AS:

- Tape recorders provide a way to record messages and information that can be listened to later, at a less demanding time.

- Auditory trainers can be useful for people who struggle to separate environmental sounds from the voice or other sounds that they want to listen to. In this case auditory trainers are not used for amplification, but to filter out external sounds.

- Electronic organizers can be helpful for those who have difficulty remembering their schedules and assignments.

- Hand-held dictionaries are useful. Talking dictionaries can be even more useful for persons who have difficulty reading or spelling.

High-tech devices for persons with AS:

- Alternative keyboards come in many sizes and configurations. For example, keyboards with either large or small keys are available to accommodate a person's motor impairments. Programmable keyboards can be used for a greater degree of customization.

- Digital whiteboard devices make it possible to save and print anything that is written on a whiteboard. These devices can be useful for students who have difficulty copying notes from the board.

- Text-to-speech software enables a computer to speak digital text, very helpful to the person with reading or vision difficulties.

- Talking word-processing software provides auditory feedback that makes it easier to correct spelling and grammar errors.

- Speech recognition software allows you to speak into the computer through a microphone and have the text appear on the computer screen. The use of this type of software can involve substantial training for each user.

- Graphic organizers allow teachers and students to brainstorm and organize ideas electronically, and then view the information in various formats, such as outlines and story webs. This visual representation of information can be a useful organizational tool. This tool can also be used in the workplace.

- Electronic math templates are useful for people who have difficulty with handwriting. The software aligns the numbers correctly, making it possible to do calculations such as multiplication and long division on the computer.

DIRECT INSTRUCTION

Direct instruction is a method for teaching that emphasizes well-developed and carefully planned instruction designed around small learning increments and clearly defined and prescribed teaching tasks. This instructional approach, that is instructor-guided, has proven to be successful with children, teens, and adults with disabilities.

Guided instructional approaches have proved superior to unguided or minimally guided instructional approaches for all people, although the less guided approaches are more popular (Kirschner, Sweller and Clark 2006). The advantage of guided instruction begins to diminish only when learners have sufficiently high prior knowledge in the area to provide the internal guidance they need to learn with minimal guidance. Since disabilities often impede learning, direct or guided instruction is even more essential to the learning process.

EFFECTIVE LISTENING

Learning to become an effective listener is a difficult task for many people; however, it is especially difficult for teens or adults with AS. The good news is that the specific skills of effective listening behavior can be learned.

Effective listening requires that you give your full physical attention to the speaker. Effective listening is listening with the whole body (Bolton 1979).

Effective attending is a careful balance of alertness and relaxation that includes body movement, eye contact, and posture. Fully attending says to the speaker, "What you are saying is very important. I am totally present and intent on understanding you." We create a posture of involvement by:

- leaning gently towards the speaker

- facing the other person squarely

- maintaining an open posture with arms and legs uncrossed

- maintaining an appropriate distance between us and the speaker

- moving our bodies in response to the speaker, e.g., appropriate head nodding and facial expression.

Effective listening requires that we be aware of the speaker's nonverbal messages. When we pay attention to the speaker's body language we gain insight into how that person is feeling as well into as the intensity of the feeling. Through careful attention to body language and paralinguistic cues, we are able to develop hunches about what the speaker is communicating.

Effective listening requires that we pay attention to the words and feelings that are being expressed. In order to understand the total meaning of the message, we must be able to gain understanding about both the feeling and the content of the message. We are often more comfortable dealing with the content than the feelings part of the message, particularly when the feelings are intense; however, for the person with AS it becomes even more complicated because he or she may not be able to interpret the feelings correctly. If this is the case then the next step in effective listening will serve you well.

Effective listening also requires the use of reflective listening. Reflective listening or responding is the process of restating, in our own words, the feeling or content that is being expressed. By reflecting back to the speaker what we believe that we understand, we validate that person by giving him the experience of being heard and acknowledged. We also provide an opportunity for the speaker to give us feedback about the accuracy of our perceptions, thereby increasing the effectiveness of our overall communication.

Effective listening also requires that we avoid verbal and nonverbal communication barriers. Verbal communication barriers include attacking a person by interrogating, criticizing, blaming, and shaming; sending "you" messages that include moralizing, preaching, advising, and diagnosing; showing power by ordering, threatening, commanding, and directing; and other verbal barriers such as shouting, name calling, and refusing to speak.

Nonverbal communication barriers including flashing or rolling eyes, quick or slow movements, arms or legs crossed, gestures made with exasperation, slouching or hunching over, poor personal self-care, doodling, staring at people or avoiding eye contact, and excessive fidgeting with materials. Several of the nonverbal communication barriers may be difficult for persons with AS to avoid, such as not giving eye contact and excessive fidgeting with materials. If eye contact is problematic then practicing eye gaze may be a good alternative.

EYE GAZE

Eye gaze is a modified form of making eye contact with another person. Eye gaze is when you look around or past a person's face and then for a short interval gaze across the face of the person catching her eyes for just a moment and then moving on to the side again. Eye contact is looking directly into the eyes of another person. This behavior is typically difficult for persons with AS and can be highly anxiety producing. For this reason eye gaze may be an acceptable alternative.

Eye contact emotionally communicates to the other person that you see him, acknowledge him, are attending to him and, in essence, view him as significant. When eye contact is missing from a social interaction, the person needing eye contact feels dismissed or neglected. His social needs are not met by the listener when eye contact is not returned. The predicament is that, for the listener, giving direct eye contact is painful. Eye gaze might just be the next best thing. Eye gaze gives the communication partner what he needs, acknowledgment without causing too much stress to the teenager or adult with AS.

FIX-UP STRATEGIES

Fix-up strategies are tools or strategies that can be used to repair or correct a miscommunication. The first step in using a "fix-up" strategy effectively is to use your nonverbal observation skills to identify a miscommunication. This will be hard for many teens and adults with AS since problems identifying and interpreting nonverbal communication like facial expression is a significant part of the AS experience.

The best way to identify a miscommunication is to watch and carefully observe the facial expressions and body language of the listener while you are talking. Observing facial expressions to identify confusion in the listener will require looking at the person's eyes, but if this is just too painful you will need to use your eye gaze strategy to frequently "check-in" with your communication partner. If the person appears puzzled, confused, or has a questioning look on their face it would be good to ask if there is a problem or ask a question. This allows for early detection of a miscommunication and if a miscommunication has not occurred it still demonstrates that as a speaker you are concerned for the other person. Being concerned for the well-being of others is generally viewed as a positive social characteristic. Also, if you make a mistake it is always good to apologize, "I am sorry, I thought that I detected a problem?"

"Fix-up" strategies may include evaluating your comments to be sure that it is what you wanted to say, restating the comment with words that more carefully represent your thoughts, or asking the person what they heard you say so that you can listen to their interpretation. At that point you may apologize for the miscommunication and try again with a different approach explaining what you really meant. If you do not meet your first goal to communicate by speaking or listening clearly, the next best step every time is to apologize.

LISTS

To-do lists can be extremely helpful in helping a person with AS to get organized and complete tasks. To make the most of this strategy be sure to use the following steps:

1. Identify what is important to do.

2. Rank your tasks into the best order.

3. Consolidate the tasks on your list when possible to make the best use of your time. For example check your e-mail while drying clothes or review your morning routine while taking a shower.

4. Complete what is on your list and transfer any tasks you didn't complete to a new list for the next day. Check off the completed tasks as you go.

It is important to remember when using lists to write things down. Do not try to remember everything you need to do. Be sure to plan ahead. Do not wait until the last minute to make your list. Set deadlines for yourself and meet them. Prioritize your list by placing the most important things first. The way you determine what is important may involve the opinions of others. For example, you may not think that completing your time sheet at work is important, but your boss may think that it is the most important task on a given day, so you need to incorporate your boss's opinion into your decision making.

Be both focused and flexible. Get into the habit of using to-do lists, but do not become a slave to your lists. Allow yourself to make necessary adjustments as you go. Using lists will simplify your life and help you to feel less stressed. A good saying for using lists is "Plan your work, work your plan and allow room for the unexpected!"

NOTE-TAKING

Note-taking skills are important because they can be used by the teen or adult with AS to record her observations and reflections while working to increase her social understanding. Note-taking can also be used on the job, at school, and in the community. In order to make the most of note-taking, it is important to use good note-taking strategies. These are a few tips for taking notes:

- Record only worthwhile facts; be sure to include the name and role of the speaker and the date.

- Use your words or the speaker's words, whichever is easiest.

- Write in phrases, as short as possible.

- Listen for introductory and summary remarks.

- Listen for pointer-words, especially numbers.

- Skip examples unless needed to understand the idea.

- Use every possible abbreviation.

- Leave a blank space if you miss something; ask later.

- Write down dates, procedures, diagrams, and graphs.

- Put your comments and additional questions in brackets.

ROLE-PLAYING

Role-playing is a teaching tool that helps you learn how to respond in various social situations (Betts and Patrick 2006). Role-playing is when two or more people act out a script for the purpose of practicing new skills, and allows teens and adults to practice new skills risk-free. The scripts are typically hypothetical which allows the participants the opportunity to rehearse different roles that can help increase understanding of the values and positions held by other people.

SCRIPTS

A script will allow you to rehearse your conversation before talking with a prospective friend by increasing your comfort with the coming conversation. A script considers the conversation of the speaker and the listener. Once a script is written it can be rehearsed and modified for many different uses. A script that starts out as an external support becomes an internal with practice. Remember when writing a script to prepare questions that will require more than "yes" or "no" responses; using how, why, and where are good question starters.

You may choose to write a script that focuses on your interests alone or you may choose to include some self-disclosure. Self-disclosure is when you tell the other person about your disability for the purpose of clarifying behaviors or mannerisms that may have already revealed your difficulties. In many instances other people have already identified that a social problem exists because of the ease in which people with typical social skills detect problems with pragmatics. People typically respond well when they understand the nature of the problem.

SELF-ASSESSMENT

Self-assessment is an essential capability for all people. It is through self-assessment and examination that we can get to a place where we begin to identify areas that we want to change or modify in our lives. For the person with AS who has a desire to change in the area of social relationships, self-assessment in this area can guide planning.

Self-assessment is used in organizations, businesses, and education to discern strengths and the areas in which improvements can be made. Self-assessment culminates with a plan for improvement along with specific actions that will be used to monitor progress.

Many different tools can be used for completing a self-assessment including rating scales, checklists, questionnaires, and personal journals. The self-assessment tool selected for this book is a rating scale that is designed to establish a baseline of strengths and weaknesses in the specific behaviors required for effective social interaction. The purpose of the rating scale is to guide the reader through an activity of self-examination; it is not for diagnostic purposes. The results of the self-assessment can be used to determine which areas of social relatedness to address first.

SELF-DETERMINATION

Self-determination is important for all people, with or without disabilities, and regardless of the type or severity of the disability.

> Self-determination is a combination of skills, knowledge, and beliefs that enable a person to engage in goal-directed, self-regulated and autonomous behavior. An understanding of your strengths and limitations together with a belief in yourself as capable and effective are essential to self-determination. When acting on the basis of these skills and attitudes, individuals have greater ability to take control of their lives and assume the role of successful adults. (Field *et al.* 1998, p.2)

Skills in self-determination benefit everyone when used in a manner that appropriately matches the person's needs, interests, and goals. For example, a person with more significant needs may express his self-determination by choosing a living arrangement that is suited for his needs after visiting several places. Similarly, college-bound high school students may exhibit self-determination by selecting a college that matches their interests and strengths.

The knowledge, skills, and beliefs needed for self-determination are not generally learned informally by people with disabilities. The skills and attitudes must be taught through direct instruction paired with opportunities for practice. This instruction usually takes place during the transition from high school to work, but can be taught at any time in life. It is never too late to embrace the skills and beliefs of self-determination.

The purpose of self-determination is to allow an individual greater control of his or her life. For this to be successful it is essential to learn how to make good decisions. The specific capabilities that are essential for good decision making in the area of career and vocation include:

- the ability to plan for near and distant futures

- the ability to take control of your own life

- a healthy self-esteem

- the ability and willingness to explore careers and opportunities

- the willingness to ask questions and seek solutions

- the willingness to seek out and use resources

- the willingness to participate in school-based and community-based activities.

The specific capabilities that are essential for good decision making in the area of living arrangements are exactly the same, so developing all seven capabilities will be a big step toward your goal of greater independence.

SELF-DISCLOSURE

Self-disclosure is when you tell another person that you have a disability. It can be difficult to know when to tell others and when not to tell. Some reasons to disclose may be to enlist understanding from a teacher or employer who is responsible for extending school or work accommodations or to a prospective friend who might understand and tolerate your behavior better if they knew that the behaviors resulted from a disability. A good reason not to disclose would be fear of discrimination.

For some people the actual disclosure is not an issue because the disability is visually identifiable, but for those with AS this is not generally the case. AS in most cases is an invisible disability. For those with visually identifiable disabilities the issue of self-disclosure becomes one of how much to disclose. The dilemma for the teen and adult with AS is whether to disclose and how much to disclose.

The answer to that question will depend upon the nature of the relationship. If a relationship falls into the category of acquaintance like a teacher or an employer you may choose to tell only the specific diagnosis and the accommodations you require to access the school curriculum or employment. Acquaintances typically do not need or want to know the nature and severity of your personal struggles. This goes beyond the scope of that kind of relationship.

If a relationship falls into the category of a friendship you may over time choose to share information about your disability in greater detail. In this type of relationship there is a commitment to care about the other person, increasing the likelihood that the friend can be trusted with the information. Remember that friends are often very accommodating to the difficulties of friends, but are generally not willing or qualified to serve as a therapist. It is better to share the essentials with your friend and leave the chronic or heavy emotional difficulties for a therapist or counselor.

In conversations, acquaintances and friends will often take turns sharing personal information to learn more about each other and develop rapport. One person may elicit information from another either by asking direct questions or by disclosing personal information in the hopes of getting the other person to disclose similar information. You will need to decide whether the question or the direction of the conversation is something that you feel comfortable with. Remember that it is perfectly acceptable for you to refrain from answering a personal question that makes you uncomfortable or to change the topic of conversation.

My Journal

PERSONAL RATING SCALE

Directions

Read each statement and check the box below that most accurately describes how you view yourself. Place the number for the checked box on the line at the end of each row.

Example: I like pizza.

☒ Strongly Agree (4)   ❑ Agree (3)   ❑ Disagree (2)   ❑ Strongly Disagree (1) <u>4</u>

1. I am a good listener.

❑ Strongly Agree (4)   ❑ Agree (3)   ❑ Disagree (2)   ❑ Strongly Disagree (1) __

2. I have a good attention span.

❑ Strongly Agree (4)   ❑ Agree (3)   ❑ Disagree (2)   ❑ Strongly Disagree (1) __

3. I notice people around me.

❑ Strongly Agree (4)   ❑ Agree (3)   ❑ Disagree (2)   ❑ Strongly Disagree (1) __

4. I have good manners.

❑ Strongly Agree (4)   ❑ Agree (3)   ❑ Disagree (2)   ❑ Strongly Disagree (1) __

5. I know when people are upset with me even when they do not say a word.

❑ Strongly Agree (4)   ❑ Agree (3)   ❑ Disagree (2)   ❑ Strongly Disagree (1) __

6. Other people understand what I say.

❑ Strongly Agree (4)   ❑ Agree (3)   ❑ Disagree (2)   ❑ Strongly Disagree (1) __

7. I request information from others.

❑ Strongly Agree (4)   ❑ Agree (3)   ❑ Disagree (2)   ❑ Strongly Disagree (1) __

8. I use appropriate volume, rate and inflection in my speech.

❑ Strongly Agree (4)   ❑ Agree (3)   ❑ Disagree (2)   ❑ Strongly Disagree (1) __

9. I like people.

❑ Strongly Agree (4)   ❑ Agree (3)   ❑ Disagree (2)   ❑ Strongly Disagree (1) __

10. I feel like crying when others are hurting.

❑ Strongly Agree (4)   ❑ Agree (3)   ❑ Disagree (2)   ❑ Strongly Disagree (1) __

11. I like talking to strangers.

❑ Strongly Agree (4)   ❑ Agree (3)   ❑ Disagree (2)   ❑ Strongly Disagree (1) __

12. I remember other people's names.

❑ Strongly Agree (4)   ❑ Agree (3)   ❑ Disagree (2)   ❑ Strongly Disagree (1) __

13. I get along well with others.

❑ Strongly Agree (4)   ❑ Agree (3)   ❑ Disagree (2)   ❑ Strongly Disagree (1) __

14. I like telling people about myself.

❑ Strongly Agree (4)   ❑ Agree (3)   ❑ Disagree (2)   ❑ Strongly Disagree (1) __

15. I notice when people are missing or away.

❑ Strongly Agree (4)   ❑ Agree (3)   ❑ Disagree (2)   ❑ Strongly Disagree (1) __

16. I have friends.

❑ Strongly Agree (4)   ❑ Agree (3)   ❑ Disagree (2)   ❑ Strongly Disagree (1) __

17. I express my feelings.

❑ Strongly Agree (4)   ❑ Agree (3)   ❑ Disagree (2)   ❑ Strongly Disagree (1) __

18. I can handle conflict.

❑ Strongly Agree (4)   ❑ Agree (3)   ❑ Disagree (2)   ❑ Strongly Disagree (1) __

19. I understand what other people want.

❑ Strongly Agree (4)   ❑ Agree (3)   ❑ Disagree (2)   ❑ Strongly Disagree (1) __

20. I keep my feet and hands to myself.

❑ Strongly Agree (4)   ❑ Agree (3)   ❑ Disagree (2)   ❑ Strongly Disagree (1) __

21. I like parties.

❑ Strongly Agree (4)   ❑ Agree (3)   ❑ Disagree (2)   ❑ Strongly Disagree (1) __

22. I speak clearly.

❑ Strongly Agree (4)   ❑ Agree (3)   ❑ Disagree (2)   ❑ Strongly Disagree (1) __

23. I feel sorry for some people.

❑ Strongly Agree (4)   ❑ Agree (3)   ❑ Disagree (2)   ❑ Strongly Disagree (1) __

24. I understand what other people say.

❑ Strongly Agree (4)   ❑ Agree (3)   ❑ Disagree (2)   ❑ Strongly Disagree (1) __

Calculating results

Transfer the number values from each statement on the Personal Rating Scale to the corresponding category. For example if you gave yourself a 2 for the first question "I am a good listener" then you would place the number 2 in the category entitled "self-regulation." Complete this process until your rating for every question has been placed in the correct category. Next add the number values for each category. After determining the total for each category divide the total number by the total number of possible points. For example if your total number of points in the Self-regulation Skills category is 8 and the total possible points is 12 you would divide 12 by 8 getting a percentage of possible points which in this case is 66 percent. The answer is the percentage of possible points you have assigned yourself for each area. Complete this calculation for each category. Transfer the percentages for each category to the Results and Interpretation Summary.

Observation skills (3, 12, 15)

___

___ Total ___/12

___ __ ÷ 12 = ___

Social skills (4, 9, 13, 16, 21)

___

___ Total ___/20

___ __ ÷ 20 = ___

___

___

Empathy (10, 19, 23)

___

___ Total ___/12

___ __ ÷ 12 = ___

Self-regulation skills (2, 18, 20)

___

___ Total ___/12

___ __ ÷ 12 = ___

Listening skills (1, 5, 24)

___

___ Total ___/12

___ __ ÷ 12 = ___

Conversational skills (7, 11, 14, 17)

___

___ Total ___/16

___ __ ÷ 16 = ___

___

Speech skills (6, 8, 22)

___

___ Total ___/12

___ __ ÷ 12 = ___

Results and interpretation summary

	Percentage	Descriptor*
Conversational skills	____	_____
Empathy	____	_____
Listening skills	____	_____
Observation skills	____	_____
Self-regulation skills	____	_____
Social skills	____	_____
Speech skills	____	_____

*See list of descriptors below.

Self-assessment descriptor key

Percentage	Descriptor
0 to 25%	Profound inhibitor—current skills likely to have a profound negative impact on social relationships
26% to 50%	Severe inhibitor—current skills likely to have a severe negative impact on social relationships
51% to 75%	Moderate inhibitor—current skills likely to have a moderate negative impact on social relationships
76% to 100%	Acceptable—current skills likely to have a positive impact on social relationships

Sample rating scale

1. I am a good listener.

☐ Strongly Agree (4)　☒ Agree (3)　☐ Disagree (2)　☐ Strongly Disagree (1) _3_

2. I have a good attention span.

☐ Strongly Agree (4)　☐ Agree (3)　☒ Disagree (2)　☐ Strongly Disagree (1) _2_

3. I notice people around me.

☐ Strongly Agree (4)　☒ Agree (3)　☐ Disagree (2)　☐ Strongly Disagree (1) _3_

4. I have good manners.

☐ Strongly Agree (4)　☒ Agree (3)　☐ Disagree (2)　☐ Strongly Disagree (1) _3_

5. I know when people are upset with me even when they do not say a word.

☐ Strongly Agree (4)　☐ Agree (3)　☒ Disagree (2)　☐ Strongly Disagree (1) _2_

6. Other people understand what I say.

☐ Strongly Agree (4)　☐ Agree (3)　☒ Disagree (2)　☐ Strongly Disagree (1) _2_

7. I request information from others.

☐ Strongly Agree (4)　☐ Agree (3)　☒ Disagree (2)　☐ Strongly Disagree (1) _2_

8. I use appropriate volume, rate and inflection in my speech.

☐ Strongly Agree (4)　☒ Agree (3)　☐ Disagree (2)　☐ Strongly Disagree (1) _3_

9. I like people.

☐ Strongly Agree (4)　☐ Agree (3)　☒ Disagree (2)　☐ Strongly Disagree (1) _2_

10. I feel like crying when others are hurting.

❏ Strongly Agree (4)   ❏ Agree (3)   ☒ Disagree (2)   ❏ Strongly Disagree (1) 2̲

11. I like talking to strangers.

❏ Strongly Agree (4)   ❏ Agree (3)   ☒ Disagree (2)   ❏ Strongly Disagree (1) 2̲

12. I remember other people's names.

❏ Strongly Agree (4)   ❏ Agree (3)   ❏ Disagree (2)   ☒ Strongly Disagree (1) 1̲

13. I get along well with others.

❏ Strongly Agree (4)   ☒ Agree (3)   ❏ Disagree (2)   ❏ Strongly Disagree (1) 3̲

14. I like telling people about myself.

❏ Strongly Agree (4)   ❏ Agree (3)   ☒ Disagree (2)   ❏ Strongly Disagree (1) 2̲

15. I notice when people are missing or away.

❏ Strongly Agree (4)   ❏ Agree (3)   ❏ Disagree (2)   ☒ Strongly Disagree (1) 1̲

16. I have friends.

❏ Strongly Agree (4)   ❏ Agree (3)   ☒ Disagree (2)   ❏ Strongly Disagree (1) 2̲

17. I express my feelings.

❏ Strongly Agree (4)   ❏ Agree (3)   ☒ Disagree (2)   ❏ Strongly Disagree (1) 2̲

18. I can handle conflict.

❏ Strongly Agree (4)   ❏ Agree (3)   ☒ Disagree (2)   ❏ Strongly Disagree (1) 2̲

19. I understand what other people want.

❏ Strongly Agree (4)   ☒ Agree (3)   ❏ Disagree (2)   ❏ Strongly Disagree (1) 3̲

20. I keep my feet and hands to myself.

☒ Strongly Agree (4)   ❑ Agree (3)   ❑ Disagree (2)   ❑ Strongly Disagree (1) _4_

21. I like parties.

❑ Strongly Agree (4)   ❑ Agree (3)   ❑ Disagree (2)   ☒ Strongly Disagree (1) _1_

22. I speak clearly.

❑ Strongly Agree (4)   ☒ Agree (3)   ❑ Disagree (2)   ❑ Strongly Disagree (1) _3_

23. I feel sorry for some people.

❑ Strongly Agree (4)   ☒ Agree (3)   ❑ Disagree (2)   ❑ Strongly Disagree (1) _3_

24. I understand what people say.

❑ Strongly Agree (4)   ❑ Agree (3)   ☒ Disagree (2)   ❑ Strongly Disagree (1) _2_

Sample result calculation

Transfer the number values from each statement on the Personal Rating Scale to the corresponding category. For example if you gave yourself a 2 for the first question "I am a good listener" then you would place the number 2 in the category entitled "self-regulation." Complete this process until your rating for every question has been placed in the correct category. Next add the number values for each category. After determining the total for each category divide the total number by the total number of possible points. For example if your total number of points in the Self-regulation Skills category is 8 and the total possible points is 12 you would divide 12 by 8 getting a percentage of possible points which in this case is 66 percent. The answer is the percentage of possible points you have assigned yourself for each area. Complete this calculation for each category. Transfer the percentages for each category to the Results and Interpretation Summary

Observation skills (3, 12, 15)

_3_

_1_ Total 5 / 12

_1_ 5 ÷ 12 = 0.42 or 42 %

Social skills (4, 9, 13, 16, 21)

_3_

_2_ Total 11 / 20

_3_ 11 ÷ 20 = 0.55 or 55%

_2_

_1_

Empathy (10, 19, 23)

_2_

_3_ Total 8 / 12

_3_ 8 ÷ 12 = 0.66 or 66%

Self-regulation skills (2, 18, 20)

_2_

_2_ Total 8 / 12

_4_   8 ÷ 12 = 0.66 or 66%

Listening skills (1, 5, 24)

_3_

_2_ Total 7 / 12

_2_ 7 ÷ 12 = 0.58 or 58%

Conversation skills (7, 11, 14, 17)

_2_

_2_ Total 8 / 16

_2_ 8 ÷ 16 = 0.50 or 50%

_2_

Speech skills (6, 8, 22)

_2_

_3_ Total 8 / 12

_3_ 8 ÷ 12 = 0.66 or 66%

Sample results and interpretation summary

	Percentage	Descriptor
Conversation skills	50%	moderate inhibitor
Empathy	66%	moderate inhibitor
Listening skills	58%	moderate inhibitor
Observation skills	42%	severe inhibitor
Self-regulation skills	66%	moderate inhibitor
Social skills	55%	moderate inhibitor
Speech skills	66%	moderate inhibitor

WOULD I MAKE A GOOD FRIEND?

Read and think about each statement. Then circle either "yes" or "no" to identify the answer that best describes you.

- I am cooperative.   Yes or No

- I am a good listener.   Yes or No

- I like to talk to other people.   Yes or No

- I am helpful.   Yes or No

- I share my possessions with others.   Yes or No

- I share my time with others.   Yes or No

- I would help a friend even if I would
  rather be doing something else.   Yes or No

- I would allow my friend to have their
  own opinions without getting mad.   Yes or No

- I can be trusted to keep secrets.   Yes or No

- I would give helpful advice to my friend
  without being bossy.   Yes or No

- I could take advice from my friend
  without getting mad.   Yes or No

- I would support my friend if they had
  a problem.   Yes or No

- I would make a good friend.   Yes or No

PERSONAL INTEREST SURVEY

Circle the activities on this list that you enjoy. Then rank the activities you circled from 1 to 15 with 1 being your most favorite and 15 being your least favorite.

Activity or Interest	*Rating 1 to 15*
Attending church	_____
Bike riding	_____
Computer time	_____
Cooking	_____
Eating in restaurants	_____
Hobbies	_____
Pets	_____
Playing sports	_____
Playing video/computer games	_____
Reading	_____
Swimming	_____
Walking	_____
Viewing movies	_____
Watching sports	_____
Writing	_____
Other _____	_____

LISTS AND SCRIPTS

Lists are bulleted or numbered topics or fact to remember and follow when talking to another person. Lists can be used effectively in conversations with acquaintances or at the starting point of a friendship.

Example list

This list would be used to guide your conversation in asking someone to attend a soccer match.

- Greeting.
    - Hello, good to see you again.
    - Hi, how are you today?
- A little small talk.
    - How are you? or How have you been?
    - What have you been up to lately?
- Introducing the topic
    - Do you like sport?
    - Are you a soccer fan?
- Asking the question
    - Do you ever go to matches?
        - If yes: I have two tickets to a match next Saturday, it would be great if you could go with me.
        - If no: You would probably have a great time, I have two tickets to a match next Saturday, it would be great if you would do with me. It is fun!

Scripts are similar to lists, yet more prescriptive. When writing a script try to use questions that require more than a "yes" or "no" response; using how, why, and where are good question starters.

Example script

You:	Hi Marty! (wait for a response)
Marty:	Hi!
You:	I heard that you are interested in World Cup soccer, is that true?
Marty:	Yes.
You:	Have you been watching the tournament?
Marty:	Yes.
You:	Who is your favorite team?
Marty:	England.
You:	Mine too, how do you think they are doing?
Marty:	I am very pleased with their play.
You:	How did you get to like soccer?
Marty:	I played when I was a kid and now all of my kids play.
You:	Great! I am trying to get a few people together for the game next week, are you free? If not, then how about the final game?
Marty:	I am busy next week, but I could make the final. Here's my number, just call.
You:	Good, I will call, bye.

AN HONEST APPRAISAL

Directions

Answer each of the following questions about your communication skills, be honest! Use the responses to evaluate your effectiveness as a speaker and listener. Use your new insight into your communication skills to guide you to becoming a better communicator.

As the speaker

- I want the listener to understand my message.

- I speak clearly.

- I am able to maintain the topic of conversation.

- I use transition statements when changing topics during a conversation.

- I watch the listener and look for signals that I am being understood.

- If I detect a problem I will attempt to modify my speech.

- If the modification does not work I will ask the person if they are following me.

As the listener

- I extend my full attention to the speaker.

- I try to provide the speaker with signals such as eye contact or eye gaze so that they know that I am paying attention.

- I refrain from interrupting.

- I wait my turn to respond.

- I refrain from formulating my response while the other person is speaking.

- If I do not understand the speaker I will ask for clarification.

- To assure understanding I will ask the person if I can rephrase what they just said.

WHAT ABOUT DATING?

Directions

Think about dating as it relates to you and answer the following questions. Use the answers to help define the dating relationship that is best for you.

1. List your personal interests and hobbies.

2. How do you prefer to spend your time?

3. Is there time in your schedule for dating?

4. If so, how much time?

5. What do you have to offer someone who you might date?

6. Would you prefer to date for companionship?

7. Would you prefer to date for a romantic relationship?

8. Would you prefer to date one person exclusively?

9. Would you prefer someone to date you exclusively?

10. Do you want to get married?

11. Do you want to have children?

12. Would you prefer to date someone gradually over a long period of time?

13. If so, how would you communicate this to your date and potential partner?

14. Do you want to disclose your AS to the person you date?

15. If so, how do you think that you would accomplish this?

16. What would you predict could be the biggest hurdle when dating?

17. How might you overcome this hurdle?

PERSONAL RULES FOR SAFETY

Directions

List the places you spend time. Suggestions include home, work, and school, on the computer, shopping mall, grocery store, doctor's office, or gym. Write several personal rules for safety regarding strangers for each place.

Examples

Home:

1. Do not open the door for strangers if at home alone.

2. Do not give personal information to a stranger on the telephone.

Computer:

1. Do not give any personal or financial information out on the internet.

2. Do not meet with a stranger from the internet.

3. Tell someone if a stranger attempts to contact you on the internet.

_____

_____

_____

_____

_____

_____

_____

BEHAVIOR AS COMMUNICATION

Directions

Observe and note the verbal and nonverbal behaviors of your child. Recording his or her behaviors will allow you to begin to identify patterns of communication that will make it easier to interpret future behaviors. It would be useful to note desirable and undesirable behaviors. Be sure to include in your observation what took place right before the observation period and right after the observation period.

Example

Sally was very cranky at breakfast this morning. This is a new behavior because she is usually happy. She cried loudly as if she were mad. She pushed away her food and threw back her head. Before I placed her in her high chair I remember that she pointed to the cupboard as if she was asking for something. I told her that she had to stop crying or I would have to put her down. She cried more so I put her down. She stopped crying and went straight to the cupboard and pointed again. I discovered that she was asking for noodles for breakfast and she was having her first tantrum trying to communicate her want for breakfast.

_____

_____

_____

_____

_____

_____

_____

_____

_____

_____

_____

_____

_____

_____

_____

_____

_____

_____

GUIDE FOR OBSERVING BODY LANGUAGE

Directions

While watching a movie or television program with a friend or family member select two actors to observe for a 10 or 15-minute time span. Select one character that represents the "good" one in the story and one character that represents the "bad" one in the story. Conduct separate observations and compare observations at the end of the selected time span. Refer to the section in the book on nonverbal communication for a refresher (p.52).

Observation: protagonist, main character, or the "good" one

Facial expressions communicate the following emotions:

_____

_____

_____

_____

Body postures communicate the following information:

_____

_____

_____

_____

Words communicate the following information:

_____

_____

_____

Observation: antagonist, opponent, villain, or "bad" one

Facial expressions communicate the following emotions:

_____

_____

_____

_____

Body postures communicate the following information:

_____

_____

_____

_____

Words communicate the following information:

_____

_____

_____

_____

Were there inconsistencies in the behavior or communication of either the protagonist or antagonist? If so, list the inconsistencies.

_____

_____

_____

_____

What other observations did you make?

_____

_____

_____

_____

STEPS TO HEALTHY LIVING: NUTRITION AND FITNESS

Directions

Record your food and beverage intake each day for seven days. Record the type of fitness and the number of minutes of exercise each day for seven days.

Date	Morning	Mid-day	Evening	Night	Fitness

STEPS TO HEALTHY LIVING: SLEEP SCHEDULE

Directions

Record the time into bed, the approximate length of time it took to get to sleep each night, an estimate of how many times you awakened and the actual time out of bed in the morning. Calculate the total hours of sleep by subtracting the time out of bed from the time into bed.

Date	Time into bed	How long to fall asleep? (estimate)	How many times did you awaken? (estimate)	Time out of bed	Total hours of sleep

LIVING ARRANGEMENTS

Directions

Read each statement and circle the response that reflects your opinion.

1. I would like to live in my own place.   Yes or No

2. I prefer to live alone.   Yes or No

3. I prefer to live with others.   Yes or No

4. I am able to care for myself.   Yes or No

5. I am able to care for my belongings.   Yes or No

6. I am able to manage my finances.   Yes or No

7. I am able to drive or use public transportation.   Yes or No

8. I can communicate for myself.   Yes or No

9. I am employed.   Yes or No

10. I receive financial assistance.   Yes or No

11. I would like to rent an apartment.   Yes or No

12. I will need some support to live alone.   Yes or No

If you would like to live on your own and think that you would benefit from support list the supports that you need.

_____

_____

_____

_____

HYGIENE AND GROOMING

Are people who appear clean held in high regard? Are there a lot of commercial and advertisements for soap, bathing, spas, skin care, and laundry detergent? Are there common sayings for cleanliness like, "Cleanliness is next to godliness?" Is cleanliness or lack of cleanliness something that is frequently talked about? Are unkempt people associated with other undesirable traits? If you do not adhere to the hygiene norm what do you think the cost is for you?

_____

_____

List the observed characteristics of a well-groomed individual in your culture.

_____

_____

How would you compare yourself to them.

_____

_____

Now that you have compared your style of grooming to those you have observed do you see any reason to change or modify your grooming habits? Make a list of what you would change, then list how you might accomplish these goals.

_____

_____

What are the benefits for those people and what do you think the cost might be for a person who is not well-groomed?

_____

_____

SENSORY CHALLENGES

Directions

List your sensory challenges followed by a description of the accommodations that you use that to help you cope with bathing, dressing, and grooming.

Examples

Sensory challenge: Highly sensitive to noise from shearers frequently used when getting a hair cut.

Accommodation: I try to avoid getting my hair cut, but that causes me to look unkempt or messy. I need to identify a barber who will cut my hair using scissor rather than an electric shearer.

Sensory challenge:I have a strong sensitivity to the smell of perfume. This causes me to avoid using lotions and deodorant. Other people tell me that I smell bad sometimes, especially in the warm weather.

Accommodation: Sometimes I apply unscented talcum powder to my underarms and I shower every day to slow the growth of smelly bacteria.

Sensory challenge: _____

Accommodation: _____

Sensory challenge: _____

Accommodation: _____

Sensory challenge: _____

Accommodation: _____

HOME FURNISHINGS

Directions

List the home furnishing that you think you will need for each room.
Color-code the list. Select one color to represent the items that you
already have and a second color for those items that you do not have,
yet need before moving.

Example

Kitchen: table and chairs; cutlery; pots and pans; utensils; plates and
bowls; dustpan and brush; microwave; cleaning supplies; pot holders;
hand towels and food.

Kitchen: _____

_____

_____

Bathroom:_____

_____

_____

Living room:_____

_____

_____

Dining room: _____

_____

_____

Bedroom: _____

_____

_____

PERSONAL SPENDING PLAN

Directions

1. Set up categories for your expenses that fit your lifestyle.

2. Calculate budget amounts for each of the categories; you can use pay stubs, receipts, payment books, and cancelled checks to determine these amounts.

3. Record your exact expenses in each category for the month. Use a small notebook, personal planner, or electronic PDA to keep track of your expenses. Be sure to write everything down.

4. At the end of each month determine your status in each category. Are you spending too much or have you allocated too much to each category. Remember that you may spend more or less money on a certain category in a given month so set the budget to be a little flexible. Analyze your progress, set goals, and make adjustments as necessary.

5. In the event that you are spending too much you will either have to increase your income or decrease spending. If you have debt that is hurting your spending plan you may choose to work overtime for a short period or take a second part-time job to resolve the debt. Be sure not to get in that situation again.

Sample spending plan

Categories	Budget	Actual expense	Difference
Monthly income	2,000	1,904	+96
Taxes	280	280	0
Savings	100	100	0
Expenses			
Rent	420	420	0
Utilities	150	180	-30
Food	380	400	-20
Health & medical	50	30	+20
Public transportation	150	140	+10
Debt repayment	0	0	0
Entertainment	75	100	-25
Pets	0	0	0
Clothing	100	85	+15
Miscellaneous			
Toiletries/household	80	84	-4
Gifts and donations	40	45	-5
Grooming	50	40	+10

PLANNING FOR POSTSECONDARY EDUCATION
Directions

Answer each question and write the reason for each response.

Do you see yourself attending college, university, trade school or an apprenticeship?

_____

_____

Would you prefer to attend a program while living at home or living at the college, university, trade school or in an apprenticeship?

_____

_____

Do you require special living arrangements like a private room, specialized diet, or room located in close proximity to classrooms?

_____

_____

Do you require additional academic supports others than those generally provided to all students like a tutor, academic accommodations, extended time for tests, to have notes provided for you, or a structured course syllabus?

_____

_____

Do you require social supports other than those generally provided to all students like a social skills group, a social mentor, counselling services or modified social expectations for organized school activities?

_____

_____

Are your sensory needs significant enough to warrant accommodations like sensitivities to noise, certain odors, fragrances, light, movement, texture or taste?

_____

_____

Glossary

Assistive Technology Device: any item, piece of equipment, or product system, whether acquired commercially off the shelf, modified, or customized, that is used to increase, maintain, or improve functional capabilities of a person with a disability

Augmentative communication: methods and devices that supplement existing verbal communication

Communication skills: the set of capabilities that allows people to exchange information, thoughts, attitudes, and feelings clearly and accurately

Diplomacy: subtle and skillful negotiating

Empathy: intellectually identifying with the feelings, thoughts, or attitudes of another person

Intonation: the specific voice marker that communicates certain grammatical features within a language

Language: a social, shared and agreed upon system of communication used to express and exchange ideas, thoughts, attitudes, facts, and feelings with other people

Loudness: the volume of the voice, great or small; it is measured in decibels

Monotone: a speech pattern that uses a single, unvaried pitch

Nonverbal communication: the process of communication through sending and receiving wordless messages

Observations skills: the set of capabilities used to recognize and note facts or occurrences in social surroundings

Paralinguistic cues: pitch, loudness, rhythm, stress, and intonation of the voice that are used by the speaker to emphasize communication for the purpose of providing clarity for the listener

Pitch: the sound of the voice, high or low

Pragmatics: the rules that govern the social use of language

Reciprocity: a relationship in which there is a mutual act of sending and receiving a message between two people

Rhythm: the metric pattern of speech which differs in each language

Scripts: a written dialogue and instructions for a sequence of expected behaviors

Self-advocacy: speaking or writing in support of one's self

Self-determination: making choices and decisions free from the control of others

Self-disclosure: the act or process of revealing facts and details concerning a personal situation

Self-examination: a reflective examination of one's own behavior including thoughts, motives and feelings

Social interactions: reciprocal social exchanges between people where each response is based upon the previous speaker's words or action

Social rules: the social norms that provide individual members within a society the necessary guidelines for acting and participating appropriately within the society

Social skills: the set of capabilities that are based on the social rules of any society

Stress: the emphasis placed upon words in a communication that can change the intended message dependent upon which word is stressed

Unemployed: to be jobless

Underemployment: a situation in which a worker is employed but not in the desired capacity, whether in terms of compensation, hours, or level of skill and experience

References

American Heart Association and the American College of Sports Medicine (2007) *Guidelines on Physical Activity*. Available at www.americanheart.org /presenter.jhtml?identifier=1200013, accessed on 13 March 2008.

American Heritage® Dictionary of the English Language (2008) "Hormones." Fourth Edition. Available at http://dictionary.reference.com/browse/hormones, accessed on 13 March 2008.

American Psychiatric Association (2000) *Diagnostic and Statistical Manual of Mental Disorders*, Fourth Edition Text Revision. Washington, DC: American Psychiatric Association.

Asperger, H. (1991) "Autistic Psychopathy in Childhood." In U. Frith (ed. and trans.) *Autism and Asperger Syndrome.* Cambridge: Cambridge University Press. (Original work published 1944.)

Baird, G., Simonoff, E., Pickles, A., Chandler, S., Loucas, T., Meldrum, D., and Charman, T. (2006) "Prevalence of disorders of the autism spectrum in a population cohort of children in South Thames: The Special Needs and Autism Project (SNAP)." *The Lancet 368*, 9531, 210–215.

Barnard, J., Harvey, V., Prior, A., and Potter, D. (2001) *Ignored or Ineligible: The Reality for Adults with Autism Spectrum Disorders.* London: National Autistic Society.

Baron-Cohen, S. (1989) "The autistic child's theory of mind: A case of specific developmental delay." *Journal of Child Psychology and Psychiatry 30*, 285–297.

Becoming Parents Program Inc. (2006) *Becoming Parents Program.* Seattle: Becoming Parents Program Inc. Available at www.becomingparents.com/, accessed on 13 March 2008.

Betts, D.E. and Patrick, N.J. (2006) *Homespun Remedies: Strategies in the Home and Community for Children with Autism Spectrum and Other Disorders.* London: Jessica Kingsley Publishers.

Bolick, T. (2001) *Asperger Syndrome and Adolescence: Helping Preteens and Teens Get Ready for the Real World.* Gloucester, MA: Fair Winds Press.

Bolton, R. (1979) *People Skills: How to Assert Yourself, Listen to Others, and Resolve Conflicts.* New York: Simon & Schuster.

Bruni, O. (2007) "Sleep architecture and NREM alterations in children and adolescents with Asperger Syndrome." *SLEEP 30*, 11, 1577–1585.

Center for Disease Control and Prevention (2007) *Prevalence of the Autism Spectrum Disorders in Multiple Areas of the United States, Surveillance Years 2000 and 2002.* Atlanta, GA: Centers for Disease Control and Prevention. Available at www.cdc.gov/ncbddd/dd/addmprevalence.htm, accessed on 13 March 2008.

Consumer Credit Counseling Services (2003) Atlanta, GA: Consumer Credit Counseling Services. Available at www.cccsatl.org/budget-counseling.asp, accessed on 8 July 2008.

Derbyshire, D. (2003) "Great physicists 'had Asperger's'." *Telegraph*, 5 January. Available at www.telegraph.co.uk/news/main.jhtml?xml=/news/2003/05/01/neins01.xml, accessed on 13 March 2008.

Field, S., Martin, J., Miller, R., Ward, M., and Wehmeyer, M. (1998) *A Practical Guide for Teaching Self-Determination.* Reston, VA: Council for Exceptional Children.

Fombonne, E., Zakarian, R., Bennett, A., Meng, L., and McLean-Heywood, D. (2006) "Pervasive developmental disorders in Montreal, Quebec, Canada: Prevalence and links with immunizations." *Pediatrics 118*, 1, 139–150.

Frith, U. (ed.) (1991) *Asperger and His Syndrome.* Cambridge: Cambridge University Press. Austin, TX: Pro-Ed.

Geller, L., and Cavanagh, J.M. (2005) *Falling Through the Cracks: Services for "High Functioning" Adults on the Autism Spectrum.* New York: Asperger Foundation. Available at www.aspfi.org/documents/FallingThroughtheCracks.pdf, accessed on 13 March 2008.

Gleason, J.B. (2001) "The Development of Language: An Overview and A Preview." In J.B. Gleason (ed.) *The Development of Language*, 5th edn. Boston: Allyn and Bacon.

Grandin, T. (1999) *Visual Thinking of a Person with Autism* [video]. Arlington, TX: Future Horizons, Inc.

Grandin, T. and Barron, S. (2005) *Unwritten Rules of Social Relationships: Decoding Social Mysteries through the Unique Perspectives of Autism.* Arlington, TX: Future Horizons, Inc.

Killgore, W.D., Balkin, T.J., and Wesenten, N.J. (2006) "Impaired decision making following 49 hr of sleep deprivation." *Journal of Sleep Research 15*, 1, 7–13.

Kirschner, P.A., Sweller, J., and Clark, R.E. (2006) "Why minimal guidance during instruction does not work: An analysis of the failure of constructivist, discovery, problem-based, experiential, and inquiry-based teaching." *Educational Psychologist 41*, 2, 75–86.

Klin, A., Volkmar, F.R., and Sparrow, S.S. (2000) *Asperger Syndrome.* New York: Guilford Press.

Kurita, H. (2006) "Disorders of autism spectrum." *The Lancet 368*, 9531, 179–181.

MacDermott, S., Williams, K., Ridley, G., Glasson, E., and Wray, J. (2006) *A Report Prepared for the Australian Advisory Board on Autism Spectrum Disorders. The Prevalence of Autism in Australia 2006. Can it be Established from Existing Data?* Forestville, NSW: Australian Advisory Board on Autism Spectrum Disorders. Available at www.autismaus.com.au/aca/pdfs/PrevalenceReport.pdf, accessed on 13 March 2008.

Mehrabian, A. (1972) *Nonverbal Communication.* Chicago, IL: Aldine-Atherton.

Muris, P., Steerneman, P., Merekelbach, H., Holdrinet, I., and Meesters, C. (1998) "Comorbid anxiety symptoms in children with pervasive developmental disorders." *Journal of Anxiety Disorders 12*, 4, 387–393.

National Healthy Marriage Resource Center (NHMRC) (2008) *What is a Healthy Marriage?* Fairfax, VA: National Healthy Marriage Resource Center. Available at www.healthymarriageinfo.org/marriage/whatishealthym.cfm, accessed on 13 March 2008.

Powell, J. (1990) *The Secret of Staying in Love.* Allen, TX: Resources for Christian Living.

Sutcliffe, R. (2004) *Figure of Speech Dictionary.* Opundo. Available at www.opundo.com/figures.php, accessed on 13 March 2008.

Tantam, D. (1991) "Asperger Syndrome in adulthood." In U. Frith (ed.) *Autism and Asperger Syndrome.* Cambridge: Cambridge University Press.

Tantam, D. and Prestwood, S. (1999) *A Mind of One's Own: A Guide to the Special Difficulties and Needs of the More Able Person with Autism or Asperger Syndrome,* 3rd edn. London: National Autistic Society.

U.S. Department of Health and Human Services (2005) *Dietary Guidelines for Americans.* Washington, D.C.: U.S. Department of Health and Human Services. Available at www.health.gov/dietaryguidelines/dga2005/document/default.htm, accessed on 13 March 2008.

Vocational Assessment (1990) *A Guide for Parents and Professionals.* Washington, D.C.: National Information Center for Children and Youth with Disabilities. Available at www.nichcy.org,pubs/outprint/tr6txt.htm, accessed on 13 March 2008. [AQ]

Wanf, J.S. and Knipling, R.R. (1994) *Single Vehicle Roadway Departure Crashes: Problem Size Assessment and Statistical Description.* Washington, D.C.: Department of Transportation (DOT HS 808 113). In Barack, P. David, G.B., and Richter, E. (1998) "The sleep of long haul truck drivers: Comment." *New England Journal of Medicine 338*, 6, 390.

Weiss, L.A., Shen, Y., Korn, J.M., Arking, D.E., Miller, D.T., Fossdal, R., Saemundsen, E., Stefansson, H., Ferreira, M., Green, T., Platt, O.S., Ruderfer, D.M., Walsh, C.A., Altshuler, D., Chakravarti, A., Tanzi, R.E., Stefansson, K., Santangelo, S.L., Gusella, J.F., Sklar, P., Wu, B., and Daly, M.J. (2008) "Association between microdeletion and microduplication at 16p11.2 and autism." *New England Journal of Medicine 358*, 7, 667–675.

Windle, R. and Warren, S. (1999) *Communication Skills.* [AQ] Eugene, OR: Consortium for Appropriate Dispute Resolution in Special Education. Available at www.directionservice.org/cadre/contents.cfm, accessed on 13 March 2008.

Winner, M.G. (2002) *Inside Out: What Makes the Person with Social Cognitive Deficits Tick?* London: Jessica Kingsley Publishers.

Winner, M.G. (2007) *Thinking About You Thinking About Me,* second edition. San Jose, CA: Think Social Publishing.

Zook, K. (2001) *Instructional Design for Classroom Teaching and Learning.* Boston: Houghton Mifflin.

Subject Index

Author Index